D0861201

LA TIERRA AMARILLA

LA TIERRA AMARILLA

Its History, Architecture, and Cultural Landscape

By Chris Wilson and David Kammer

Foreword by Robert Torrez
Preface by Thomas Merlan

Principal photography by Chris Wilson

Museum of New Mexico Press, Santa Fe

Copyright © 1989 New Mexico Historic Preservation Division. *All rights reserved*. No part of this book may be reproduced in any form or by any means without the expressed written consent of the copyright holder and the publisher.

Manufactured in the United States of America.
5   4   3   2   1

Cover design (second edition) by Linda Seals.
Maps and building plans by Caufield and Caufield
Photography by Chris Wilson unless otherwise noted

Originally published by the New Mexico Historic Preservation Division under the title *Community and Continuity: The History, Architecture and Cultural Landscape of La Tierra Amarilla*, a study financed in part by a grant from the History Preservation Fund, administered by the National Park Service, U.S. Department of the Interior, and the Historic Preservation Division, Office of Cultural Affairs, State of New Mexico. The contents and opinions do not necessarily reflect the views or policies of those agencies.

LIBRARY OF CONGRESS CATALOGING-IN-PUBLICATION DATA

Wilson, Chris (Christopher)
    [Community and continuity]
    La Tierra Amarilla : its history, architecture, and cultural landscape / by Chris Wilson and David Kammer ; foreword by Robert Torrez ; preface by Thomas Merlan ; principal photography by Chris Wilson.
        p.   cm.
    "Originally published by the New Mexico Historic Preservation Division under the title Community and continuity . . ."—T.p. verso.
    Includes bibliographical references.
    ISBN 0–89013–241–0 (pbk.)
    1. Historic buildings—Rio Chama Valley (Colo. and N.M.)
2. Vernacular architecture—Rio Chama Valley (Colo. and N.M.)
3. Rio Chama Valley (Colo. and N.M.)—Antiquities. 4. Rio Chama Valley (Colo. and N.M.)—History, Local. I. Kammer, David.
II. Title.
F802.C45W57   1992
917.89'52—dc20   92-16426
                                                                         CIP

Frontispiece: Looking east over Los Ojos to the Brazos Peaks.

Museum of New Mexico Press
P.O. Box 2087
Santa Fe, New Mexico 87504-2087

Contents

Preface

Since 1970 the State Historic Preservation Division has been conducting systematic architectural, historic and archaeological surveys of New Mexico. (These surveys are authorized by Section 101(b)(3)(A) of the National Historic Preservation Act of 1966, as amended, and by Sections 18-6-5(B) and (C) and 18-6-8(D)(3) NMSA 1978.) They are a continuation at state, local and regional levels of surveys carried out over approximately the past fifty years by the Historic American Buildings Survey, the Laboratory of Anthropology, and various private nonprofit organizations.

The object of the comprehensive survey is to identify all historically, architecturally, and archaeologically significant sites in New Mexico. The New Mexico Legislature noted in 1969 that these resources are "one of our most valued and important assets." In both cultural and economic senses, this is increasingly apparent, as tourism-related employment and revenues continue to grow, while a population mingling natives and newcomers finds continuing strength and meaning in New Mexico's culture and traditions.

Unfortunately, Federal and State legislative recognition of the importance of the program has never translated into adequate support. Although significant percentages of our cultural resources base have been documented, years of work remain to be done. New Mexico, with its long history and much longer, complex prehistory is both blessed and embarrassed by rich cultural resources which it can appreciate but neither fully understand nor adequately protect.

This study joins our series of occasional publications. It details a historic and architectural survey of a group of villages in the Chama River Valley of northwestern New Mexico.

The land grants of the short Mexican period were political and speculative, intended to encourage development of the borderlands by private initiative. They achieved this objective too late for the Mexican nation, which lost the thinly populated and undefended northern half of its territory in 1846. The development of the grants, including the Tierra Amarilla Grant, became a chapter in the expansion of the United States. Onto the subsistence farming and sheepherding economy of the Tierra Amarilla Grant the Anglo-Americans superimposed a military presence, a cash economy, and a railroad. Hispanic and Anglo-American influences joined to create the local architecture that is the subject of this study.

Money and widening markets assisted the growth of the villages, then passed them over. Conflict between traditional and communal subsistence and the modern cash economy, attended by alienation of the Grant lands, caused the decline of the communities. The historic and architectural resources recorded here, however, may play a role in revitalizing the local economy as they perpetuate the local culture.

Thomas W. Merlan, State Historic Preservation Officer

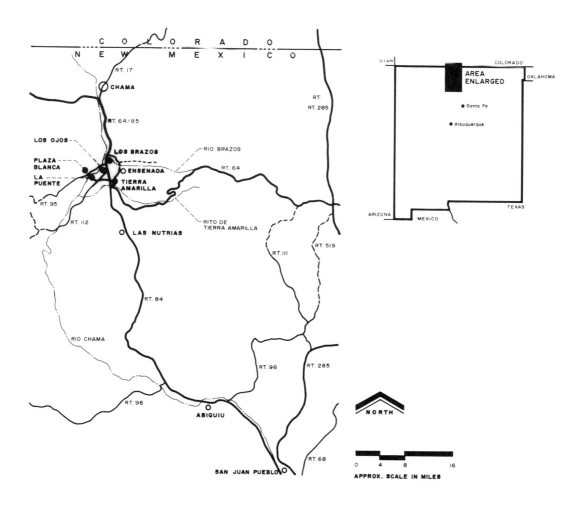

2. Location of Tierra Amarilla communities.

Introduction and Acknowledgements

As we began to survey the historic buildings of La Tierra Amarilla in the summer of 1984, some of our Albuquerque friends and acquaintances wondered if we feared for our safety. As a result of the 1967 courthouse raid, they knew of Tierra Amarilla primarily as a symbol of the land grant movement and Hispanic militancy, a place where outsiders were viewed with suspicion. Later, after studying the legal history of the local grant, we saw that there was cause for resentment. Even well-intentioned government programs designed to remedy earlier injustices frequently turned out to be mixed blessings.

When we journeyed to the area as consultants from the State Historic Preservation Division, we recognized that we came as two more in a long line of government representatives. Our first visit was made at the invitation of Los Ganados de Valle, a local economic development cooperative, which was interested in gaining historic designation for their large old commercial building, the Burns store, in Los Ojos. Later, La Sociedad Historica de la Tierra Amarilla supported the idea of a general study of area villages. Members of these groups felt that this study could only add to the community's sense of its past. Our response to our Albuquerque acquaintances became, in part, that we had been invited to do our study because community leaders saw at least a potential benefit from our work.

We were introduced around, and the word of our project spread quickly through the community grapevine. Soon people knew what these two gringos, walking the roadside, clipboard in hand, camera over the shoulder, were up to. As we talked with people on the street or over coffee at their kitchen tables, we were warmly met, generally in a reserved, courteous manner. This considerateness also became part of the story that we related to our once-concerned Albuquerque friends.

We posed nearly endless questions to local residents about past events and irrigation systems and old houses, houses that to some were due to be torn down. Some people showed a bemused tolerance for our interest in their history, or so it seemed to us. But our overwhelming sense was of a quiet pride in ancestry, in the struggle of the pioneers to settle the land, and in the on-going efforts to sustain the local cultural heritage. This estimation was confirmed when a meeting to discuss historic designation for three of the villages, held in the St. Joseph parish hall on a blizzardy night in January 1985, drew fifty people — the normal turnout for an area with ten or twenty times the population.

This study proceeded over the summers of 1984 and 1985 with the support of the Historic Preservation Division of the New Mexico Office of Cultural Affairs. As part of the state's Historic Building Inventory program, we were to document each pre-1945 building with a photograph and a one-page form of observations. In this farming area, the study was necessarily expanded to consider irrigation systems and field patterns. Library research, local interviews, and measured floor plans of representative historic buildings complemented the building inventory forms.

Gradually, from this research emerged a picture of a strong Spanish tradition underlying the ways houses were built, fields were defined and villages were laid out. Over this tradition washed waves of national popular culture, what we in New Mexico often refer to as Anglo-American influences. The subsequent blending of cultures, which is general over most of northern New Mexico, is nowhere more vivid than in the distinctive architecture of La Tierra Amarilla.

As historians, our gaze tends toward the past, an inclination reinforced in this case by our obligation to document pre-1945 buildings. We nevertheless began to recognize that the local architectural tradition is carried on today, over one hundred years after it took form. Likewise, the spirit of community cooperation coupled with determined self-reliance that characterized the Hispanic pioneers continues in the lives of many Tierra Amarilla residents today. This continuity appears in the efforts of Los Ganados del Valle, in the new bed and breakfast and restaurant in Los Brazos, or in the way people repair their own machinery and build their own houses, often using salvaged materials. We are not sociologists or economists, so our observations about recent developments, found especially in chapter four, are meant to be suggestive rather than definitive. These comments are based on the belief that preservation of historic buildings without the preservation of cultural heritage is a hollow gesture; and that cultural preservation is nearly impossible without local economic vitality. On the other hand, pride in local heritage is a powerful ally of economic development.

Our original survey led, by 1986, to the listing of five local villages, twenty-one individual structures and seven irrigation systems on the State Register of Cultural Properties and the National Register of Historic Places. Although grants-in-aid have been available for historic preservation work in the past, government preservation incentives now are primarily limited to income tax credits, from which few local residents can benefit. This book was conceived — and strongly supported by the Historic Preservation Division staff — as one way to repay part of our debt to the people of La Tierra Amarilla for their support. We also hope the book will open the area's rich cultural landscape and architecture to the sympathetic visitor, and contribute, if only modestly, to historical scholarship concerning this region.

3. Looking northeast over Tierra Amarilla to the Brazos Peaks.

The book is divided into two parts. The first gives an overview of the history, architecture and cultural geography of the area. The second part provides historical sketches and outlines driving tours of the five villages that have received historic designation, along with the complete listing of all individually registered buildings and irrigation systems. Although the authors collaborated closely, David Kammer is the primary author for chapters three through five and nine, and Chris Wilson for chapters one, two, and six through eight.

We owe a special debt of thanks to Los Ganados de Valle, to La Sociedad Historica de la Tierra Amarilla and to all those who shared their knowledge and advice or allowed us to measure their houses. Among the latter we wish to acknowledge Antonio Manzanares, Clorinda and Medardo Sanchez, Gumercindo De Vargas, Solomon Luna, Angie Serrano, Lionel Martinez, Beth Rhodes, Agapito Candelaria, Manuel Valdez, Gilbert Martinez, Cruz and Gregorita Aguilar, Jose and Asencion Torrez, Connie Peralta, Arturo Atencio, Donald Valdez, Eluterio Martinez, Adelina Valdez, Jose and Eloise Abeyta, Jose Remigio Martinez, Antonio

Lente, Jose Gabriel Abeyta, Antonio Madrid, Rafael Martinez, and, especially, Gumercindo Salazar and Maria Varela. We will never be able fully to express our gratitude to Robert Torrez for sharing with us his extensive research, which will one day yield a definitive history of La Tierra Amarilla. Our thanks also to Marc Simmons, Dan Scurlock, William deBuys, John Jackson and Peter Chestnut, who made valuable suggestions; to Carolyn Kinsman who designed the cover and advised us on the book's design; to Don Hancock who handled layout; to Mona Gonzales for typesetting; Becky Chisman for proofing; and to Mary Caufield and Jim Caufield for the fine maps and plans. And finally, our appreciation to the Historic Preservation Division staff, to Lynne Sebastian, who edited part one and the introductions, and to Thomas Merlan, Kathleen Brooker, and Mary Ann Anders without whose support and advice this project would not have been undertaken or completed.

D.J.K., C.M.W., Albuquerque, New Mexico, 1988

Mucho más antes...

*A*ny history of Tierra Amarilla needs to begin, as all settlement west of the Rio Grande along the Rio Chama began, at Abiquiu. Long before the Spanish settled New Mexico, the fertile valley along the Rio Chama had been occupied by groups of hunters and seed gatherers, some of their sites dating as far back as 3000 BC. Archeological reconnaissance has identified at least ten significant pueblo sites along the Chama between the Rio Grande and present-day Abiquiu. Although the Chama Valley has not been continuously occupied during these past 5000 years, the various occupations, abandonments and re-occupations indicate that the Chama Valley has long possessed certain attractions necessary for the protection and sustenance of its inhabitants.

The name Chama appears to have been derived from *Tsama*, the name of a pre-Spanish pueblo located on a mesa southeast of Abiquiu, whose inhabitants were related to the Indians of present-day San Juan Pueblo. The name *Tsama*, which means "wrestling place" in Tewa, may indicate that at some distant time wrestling contests were held here. The *Tsama* ruin itself shows evidence of at least three separate villages, one of which has been described by archeologist Robert Greenlee as being the earliest civilization in the Chama River valley. It is likely that the name Chama, or as the Spanish sometimes called it, Zama, referred at first to a more or less specific place, than to the Chama Valley, and ultimately to the river itself.[1]

The peoples who settled in the Chama area appear to have been descended from Indians who occupied the region along the Rio San Juan to the northwest. The Chama Valley provides a natural route for trade and communication between the Rio Grande and the San Juan region, as indicated by the patterns of mid- and late 19th century settlement expansion into present-day San Juan and northern Rio Arriba counties. Some Rio Grande Pueblo mythology suggests that the ancestors of the modern pueblo people migrated from the west by way of the San Juan drainage, Cañon Largo, and Gallinas.

The initial Chama settlements of concern to this preface occurred around the 12th century and consisted of comparatively small pueblos of between twenty and one hundred rooms, generally arranged around a plaza. Most of these were located in what might be termed "semi-defensive" sites on mesas above the river valley. Archeologist H.P. Mera suggested these sites may also have been chosen on "aesthetic impulse," but most likely their location was decided mainly to provide a measure of protection against enemies and to protect the pueblo structures themselves against dampness and floods.[2]

Archeological evidence suggests that between 1350 AD, and 1400 AD there were sizable increases in population along the Chama, probably as a result of aggregation of smaller groups living in adjacent areas into larger units in the Chama Valley. These nearby smaller pueblos appear to have been abandoned at about the same time that the larger ones appear in the archeological record, and there is little evidence to suggest that a migration from distant areas accounted for the establishment of these larger pueblos. The occupants of the large pueblos were farmers, who left evidence of a diet consisting of squash, pumpkins, beans and corn, supplemented by small game. Many of these pueblos were, in turn, abandoned during the century prior to Spanish contact.

In the early part of the 16th century, population in the Chama Valley declined abruptly, suggesting a major calamity such as nomadic raiders or deadly conflict between adjacent settlements. Archeological excavations have produced evidence of hasty abandonments at a time that coincides with the date of early Navajo contacts and influences from the west.

In 1598 the Spanish began the process of colonizing New Mexico. When Don Juan de Oñate established the Spanish settlement of San Gabriel near present-day San Juan Pueblo, the Navajo were already well established in this part of New Mexico, had adopted agriculture to some extent, and were organized in small, loosely associated bands. Some of these Navajo bands established settlements along the Chama as far east as the Piedra Lumbre region, where Abiquiu Dam is now located. Navajo presence in this area was noted by Father Geronimo Zarate-Salmeron as early as 1629. In 1634 Father Alonso Benavidez described the Navajo as being located only one day's travel from the Rio Grande pueblos.

Just as the prehistoric pueblos had used the Chama as a convenient route to the Rio Grande, these Navajo came down the Chama Valley to raid the Pueblo and Spanish settlements. Frequent retaliatory campaigns by the Spanish and their Pueblo allies passed north along the Chama, trailing Navajo raiding parties to the Piedra Lumbre and from there to the "Navajo Provinces" along the San Juan and its tributaries.

During the first decades of the 18th century, a new danger appeared on the New Mexico frontier. Utes or Yutas, as they were called by the Spanish, in particular the Capote and Wimmenuche bands, had driven the Navajo out of the upper San Juan region. By 1720 these Western Utes, some bands of Eastern Utes, and Comanches were frequently raiding Spanish settlements and Indian pueblos along the Rio Grande. These bands moved freely through the Piedra Lumbre and established camps along the Chama. One such Ute site has been identified at El Barranco near present-day Abiquiu. These were bold, energetic tribes, who dared to attack even

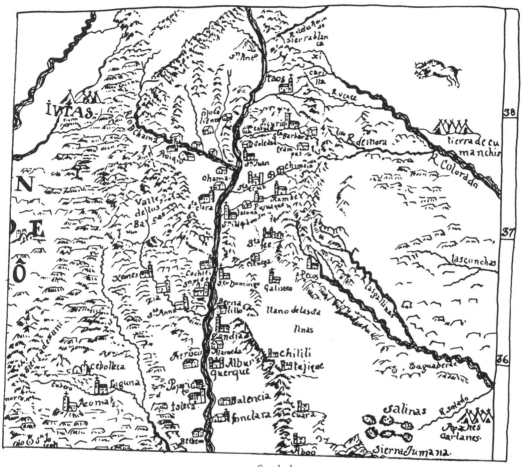

Symbols

The villas are marked	Ruined missions	
Missions · · · · · · · ·	Rancherías of Apaches and other heathens	
Presidios · · · · · · · · · ·	Roving tribes	
Settlements of Spaniards	Springs	

4. Detail of Miera map of New Mexico, about 1760. Redrawn by S. Livingston, NPS.

the major centers of Spanish settlement, as evidenced by their attack on Taos and nearby villages in 1716. In 1748, Spanish troops, led by Governor Don Joaquin Codallos y Radal, met the Comanches, and some allied Utes in a fierce battle near Abiquiu. In the course of the battle, more than one hundred Indians were killed, 200 were taken prisoner, and nearly 1000 horses were captured.

Aside from this resounding victory, little was accomplished by the Spanish during the first half of the 18th century to protect this northern frontier effectively from Indian attacks. There was almost continual conflict between the Spanish and the Utes and the Plains tribes for the balance of the century until a system of giving presents to the Utes in exchange for peace was established. The Utes were to remain a significant factor in the history of Abiquiu and Tierra Amarilla well into the 19th century.

It was during this era of conflict with the Indians that the Spanish decided to expand their frontier by allowing settlement of land along the Chama. By 1735, an expanding population in the Spanish settlements along the Rio Grande had caused crowding around Santa Cruz de la Cañada. To help to alleviate this problem, the Spanish government encouraged application for grants along the Rio Grande's tributaries, in particular the Chama. This policy not only helped to relieve crowding but also served to establish buffer settlements along the frontier which would bear the brunt of Indian attacks. The official settlement of Santa Rosa de Lima de Abiquiu began in the summer of 1734, when Bartolome Trujillo of San Jose de Chama (present-day Hernandez) petitioned the Spanish governor on behalf of himself and nine other families for a grant of land along the Rio Chama. Documentation shows that Trujillo and others had already been using the area for farming as early as 1732. The license of the chapel of Santa Rosa de Lima was issued on September 13, 1737.

For the next decade, frontier settlements such as Santa Rosa, Ojo Caliente, and Pueblo Quemado eked out a tenuous existence, with Abiquiu suffering continual Comanche and Ute attacks. In 1747 the Comanches raided Santa Rosa, killed a young girl and an old woman and carried off twenty-three women and children. Troops from Santa Fe were unable to catch the raiders, and a hastily organized group of pursuers from Santa Rosa itself found only the bodies of three women and a newborn child. It was under the pressure of mounting Indian raids that the residents of these outlying settlements finally petitioned Governor Codallos y Rabal for permission to abandon their homes and retreat to the more secure settlements until such time as the Indian menace subsided. That spring they were granted permission to move with the stipulation that they would be obliged to resettle the area as soon as the danger decreased.

In 1750, Governor Vélez Cachupin ordered the residents of Santa Rosa to return to the area and to build their homes in the customary defensive plaza. Truji and the settlers objected to this forced resettlement, but to no avail. That spring, the *Alcalde Mayor* led the reluctant settlers back to Santa Rosa. They were accompanied by a detachment of troops, who provided military protection for Indian attacks until the plaza was securely reestablished. The returning settlers were also accompanied by thirteen *genizaros*, detribalized Christian Indians, for whom the separate mission of Santo Tomas would soon be established at the present-day settlement of Abiquiu.

Governor Vélez Cachupin made a land grant to these Santa Rosa *genizaros* in 1754 and established their community on a hill west of Santa Rosa. By 1760 this new settlement of Santo Tomas de Abiquiu showed a population of fifty-seven Indian families, totaling 166 persons. Nearby Santa Rosa de Lima had now grown to one hundred families comprising 617 persons.

By 1776, Santo Tomas de Abiquiu was firmly established and had become the site of an annual trade fair, which was authorized by the Spanish government for the purpose of providing a place for the barter of goods between the Utes and the settlers. Every fall in late October and early November the Utes came to Abiquiu and exchanged deerskins, buffalo meat, and frequently, captive children for horses and corn. These children became the source of additional *genizaro* influx into the region. These *captivos*, baptised into the Catholic Faith and assimilated by their purchasers into New Mexico society, added a rich dimension to the social milieu of frontier New Mexico.

These trade fairs were also a significant factor in the development of knowledge and interest in the region north and west of Abiquiu. We have very little documentation of what the Spanish knew of the region that today is called Tierra Amarilla. The name Tierra Amarilla itself does not appear in any documents until 1820, but it is clear that by then the region was well known and probably regularly utilized by Abiquiu residents for hunting and trading with the Utes and Navajo. The first recognizable description of what we now call Tierra Amarilla was by the Franciscan Friar, Velez de Escalante, chronicler of the 1776 expedition that is also associated with the leader of the expedition, Fray Francisco Atanasio Dominguez. On August 1 of that year, Dominguez and Escalante left Abiquiu and traveled northwest in search of a practical route between Santa Fe and California. For two days they crossed through territory whose landmarks, rivers, and streams were all familiar to the Abiquiu residents as they are to present-day residents of Tierra Amarilla — Ojo del Navajo, El Rio de la Cebolla and El Rio de las Nutrias. Finally on August 3, they crossed the Rio Chama at a point somewhere between present-day Los Ojos and La Puente. They camped for the night on the west side of the river, and Escalante described the valley, with its abundant pasture and ideal location for cultivation and irrigation, as having all the things that a settlement might need "for its subsistence."

By the beginning of the 19th century, Abiquiu's expanding population began to experience a scarcity of arable land and pastures. In 1821, a census by Jose Pedro Rubi de Celis reported Santo Tomas de Abiquiu with a population of 246 Indians and 3,433 *Españoles*. In 1776, Dominguez had already noted the presence of scattered settlements to the west and north of Abiquiu. By the 1820s most of the population was located in several new settlements in the areas — Cañones, Barranco, El Rito, La Puente, San Francisco, Tierra Azul, Rio de Chama, Casita, Plaza Blanca, La Cueva, San Rafael, and Gavilan. Some of these names were subsequently duplicated at villages within La Tierra Amarilla as groups from these Abiquiu settlements moved north during the 19th century. This explanation for the duplicate settlement names is readily acknowledged by the many Tierra Amarilla residents who proudly trace their origins to these earlier frontier settlements.

Robert J. Torrez, State Historian, New Mexico Records Center and Archives

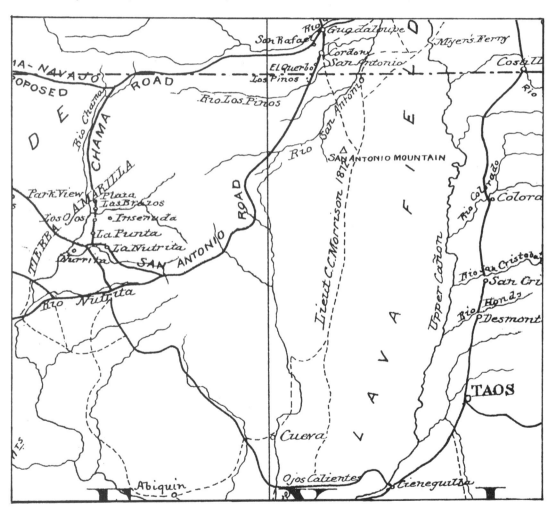

5. Detail of "Outline Map showing the lines of Communication between Southern Colorado and Northern New Mexico," By E.H. Ruffner, 1876.

1 — History & Settlement Patterns

On the first of August, 1776, a party of ten explorers led by Franciscan friars Francisco Atanasio Dominguez and Silvestre Velez de Escalante departed from the village of Abiquiu on the Spanish frontier for the wilds of Colorado and Utah. They sought an overland route between New Mexico and the recently established missions of California. Andres Muñiz, their guide, led them north over Indian trails known to him through trading with the Utes. The fourth day, at an elevation of 7300 feet, they came upon a set of mountain valleys that would come to be known early in the next century as La Tierra Amarilla — the Yellow Earth. (The name of the area was also applied to the village of Las Nutritas in 1880 when the New Mexico territorial legislature designated it as the new county seat.) Escalante, who kept the expedition's journal, described the area near present-day Los Ojos:

> The river's meadow is about a league [two and one-half miles] long
> from north to south, good land for farming with help of irrigation;
> it produces a great deal of good flax and abundant pasturage. There
> are also the other prospects which a settlement requires for its
> founding and maintenance. Here it has a good grove of white
> poplar.[1]

While Escalante was clearly alert to the possibilities for future development, the presence of hostile Indians would prevent settlement for another eighty years.

In fact, Spanish settlement had been confined to a small area along the upper Rio Grande, roughly from Albuquerque to Taos, for the almost two centuries since the first settlement in 1598. Santa Rosa de Lima, at the edge of the heavily populated Española Valley, was first settled in 1734, only to be abandoned in 1747 because of Comanche attacks. Strong pressure from the Spanish governor of New Mexico forced the settlers to reestablish the town three years later. By 1754, the *genizaro* (Hispanicized Indian) community of Santo Tomás de Abiquiu was established near-by.

Beginning about 1790, a variety of factors triggered a major expansion of Spanish settlement. A 1786 peace treaty with the Comanches lessened the intensity of nomadic Indian attacks. The availability of smallpox vaccine after 1805 led to an increase of population beyond what the Rio Grande settlements could support. The opening of the Santa Fe Trail in 1821 and the presence of the United States military after 1846 provided cash markets for local products and increased the level of protection from Indian attacks.

—

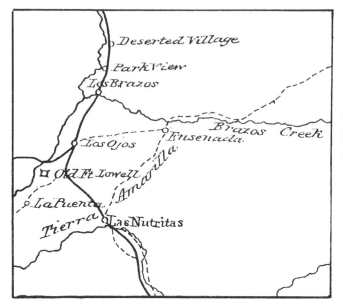

6. Detail of "Line of Communication between Conejos and Pagosa Springs, Colorado. "From C.A.H. McCauley *Report of the San Juan Reconnaissance of 1877.*

The expansion ended about 1880 as Hispanic settlers pushed up against other expanding groups: Anglo-Americans (mainly from the Midwest) to the north in Colorado, Anglo-Texans in eastern New Mexico, Chihuahuans in southern New Mexico, Navajos to the west, and Mormons to the northwest. In a little less than one hundred years, from 1790 to 1880, the area of Hispanic settlement grew tenfold and the populaton sevenfold, from approximately 12,000 to 80,000 persons. More than half of the territorial expansion occurred in the final three decades from 1850 to 1880.[2]

This settlement proceeded through what has been described as a "budding process." When the resources of a particular valley were fully allocated, surplus population spilled over into the next available irrigable valley. The summer grazing of sheep in nearby valleys gave prospective settlers first-hand knowledge of available locations. Frontier towns, such as Abiquiu, Taos and San Miguel del Bado, emerged as staging areas, places where families without their own land prepared to settle new lands.[3]

Like other frontier towns, Abiquiu also served as a buffer against Indian attack and as a trading point with Utes, Comanches and Jicarilla Apaches. By 1776, when Dominguez and Escalante passed through the village, its annual trade fair was well established. By 1829, an overland route to California, which the friars sought, was opened. Known as the Spanish Trail, it followed the old Indian trails north out of Abiquiu and through La Tierra Amarilla before turning to the west.[4]

—

It seems likely that residents of Abiquiu had begun grazing their sheep at Tierra Amarilla before 1814 when the first formal petition for a land grant there was made to the Spanish Crown. Additional petitions followed in 1820 and 1824 before a community grant was issued by the Mexican government in 1832 to a group of settlers headed by Manuel Martinez of Abiquiu. Indian raids at first prevented permanent settlement of the grant. Indeed, attacks intensified after eleven Utes visiting the governor in Santa Fe were killed in September, 1844.[5]

Although permanent settlement of La Tierra Amarilla did not occur until 1860, twelve years after New Mexico was annexed to the United States, Spanish and Mexican practices were followed in the division of the land. Traditionally, community grants were divided into three types of land: house plots in a village, irrigable fields nearby and the remaining pastures and forests held as common lands. Through the Spanish and Mexican periods, an administrative justice known as an *Alcalde* typically placed each group of settlers in possession of its grant. He helped choose and lay out the village site and assigned each family its house lot and field.

In the mountain valleys of northern New Mexico, the typical fields were fifty to 200 *varas* wide (a *vara* being about thirty-two inches). These fields stretched from the river up to the irrigation ditch. The remaining pastures and timberlands above the ditch were shared by all as community property, property that could not be

Population of Tierra Amarilla Villages[15]

Date	T.A.	Ensenada	La Puente	Los Ojos	Los Brazos	Chama
1870	163	103	84	150	71	0
1880	209	133	107	346	128	25
1890	624	w/TA	w/TA	571	w/Ojos	295
1900	607	120	117	399	200	300
1910	963	w/TA	w/TA	900	w/Ojos	733
1920	1,106	"	"	745	"	600
1930	1,097	"	"	862	"	743
1940	1,493	"	"	879	"	975
1950	1,115	"	"	656	"	1,044
1960	3,422	"	"	w/TA	w/TA	w/TA
1970	2,092	"	"	"	"	899
1980	2,022	"	"	"	"	1,090

—◀

divided or sold. Houses and fields, on the other hand, were considered private property that could be sold. If a family sold its house and fields and moved on, that family's rights to the commons and their community responsibilities also went to the new owners. Ethnohistorians Paul Kutsche and John VanNess have noted that "metaphorically, it [the family] sold out of the corporation and the new family bought in. What was bought and what was sold was not so much parcels of land as the right to live and make a living in a particular microbasin."[6] By comparison, Anglo-American custom and law view land as a salable commodity without any necessary relation to residence or community obligation.

The Laws of the Indies, issued in 1573, prescribed the form that Spanish towns and villages should take in the New World. The Laws called for a regular grid of streets, with the church and public buildings facing onto a central plaza. This compact form was realized in some of the early communities, such as Santa Fe, Albuquerque and Santa Cruz. But by the eighteenth century, as the ability of the Spanish Colonial officials to control outlying settlements decreased, a dispersed form of settlement also appeared. Although settlers were given house lots and repeatedly instructed by officials to form defensive plazas, many chose to settle near their field. Since these fields were distributed the length of each irrigated valley, sometimes extending for a distance of five or six miles, linear villages developed along common roads and trails as each family built at the edge of their field. The Spanish term *la cordillera* (the corridor) is sometimes applied to this road-side, linear village type.[7]

Historian Francis Swadish has suggested that on the northwestern New Mexico frontier, relations with nomadic Indians were responsible for dispersed settlement. This settlement form allowed settlers to protect their fields, to more easily carry out illicit trade with the Indians and to distinguish themselves from other settlers and thereby avoid attack through individually friendly relations.[8]

Although government support for Hispanic settlement patterns had disappeared by the time the Tierra Amarilla grant was occupied, Manual Martinez's son Francisco partially fulfilled the role of the *Alcalde*. He issued deeds (in Spanish *hijuelas*) to more than one hundred settlers for individual fields and for the use of the common lands.[9]

The herders who used La Tierra Amarilla before permanent settlement undoubtedly built summer camps in the area, and these seem to have formed the core of at least two of the villages established in 1860 and 1861. Oral tradition indicates that log strongholds known as *fuertes* stood in western Los Brazos (illustration 100, near buildings 123, 124, 130) and on the point south of the Los Ojos Church (illustration 94, near buildings 25-29). In each of these locations, defense was

7.Los Ojos. Photo by Paul Logsdon, 1981.

facilitated by steep hills to the south and west. As Los Brazos developed, buildings clustered together irregularly near the first stronghold, in time occupying the entire hill above the irrigated fields (illustration 99).

There are no formal plazas in any of the Tierra Amarilla villages; linear settlements predominate. The village of Ensenada, the north/south axis of Los Ojos and the long *cordillera* of Tierra Amarilla extending to the west are typical linear settlements following the edge of irrigated fields (illustration 83). La Puente and the east/west axis of Los Ojos are an alternate form of the linear village, one that runs perpendicular to the ditches and parallel to the long fields. When Francisco Martinez settled in Los Ojos, he also partially fulfilled the *Alcalde's* role by selling or disbursing town lots along a road running east/west down one of the long fields (illustration 94, buildings 1-30). Similarly, La Puente straddles a road running down the middle of a field allotment (illustration 88). Breaks in the cliffs allowing easy movement from one plateau to another contributed to the selection of locations for Los Ojos and La Puente. The core of Tierra Amarilla clusters around the intersection of two roads (illustration 61).

8. Looking west over La Puente.

Since settlers of La Tierra Amarilla were not formally placed in possession of the grant by a government official as they would have been in the Spanish or Mexican period, the exact date of permanent settlement is not documented in government records. Oral tradition and scattered written evidence support 1860 and 1861 as the years of settlement.[10] A variety of factors helped to cause and supported the move to this area. After the United States Congress confirmed the Tierra Amarilla grant in 1860, Francisco Martinez began presenting the other settlers with their deeds. Between July, 1860, and August, 1866, he distributed 122 allotments located at Los Brazos, Ensenada, Las Nutritas, Los Ojos and La Puente, as well as at two other villages, El Barranco and Cañones, which were soon abandoned because of Indian raids.[11]

Settlement was also aided by a gold rush to the San Juan Mountains of southwestern Colorado in the winter of 1860-1861. The miners following the Old Spanish Trail through the area provided some trade and road improvements. La Tierra Amarilla became a staging area for a second, more successful gold rush in 1874, which saw 500 miners pass through the villages.[12]

By the time of this second gold rush, subsistence farming and sheep herding were firmly established as the primary activities of the villagers. The threat of Indian attacks had led to the establishment of an Army post occupied from 1865 to 1869, one mile south of the village of Los Ojos. First called Camp Plummer, it was later renamed Fort Lowell. Merchants established themselves at Los Ojos during this same period. The most notable of these, Henry Mercure and T.D. Burns, competed for contracts to supply the Army. Burns later supplied the Ute Indian Agency at Las Nutritas/Tierra Amarilla (1872-1881).

A town named Park View was established in 1877 just north of Los Brazos. Conceived by land speculators in Chicago and settled primarily by Swedish immigrants, Park View never grew beyond seventy inhabitants but did introduce a grist mill and sawmill to the area. Soon after the town failed, in 1878, its post office along with the name Park View were transferred to Los Ojos. (The original name, Los Ojos, was only reinstated in 1972 by the Rio Arriba County Commission.) These developments of the 1860s and 1870s — Fort Lowell, the Indian Agency, Park View and the presence of resident merchants — began to introduce a money economy and some Anglo-American architectural practices.[13]

In 1877, Army Engineer Lt. C.A.H. McCauley made a reconnaissance of the region and reported to Congress:

> The Tierra Amarilla is the center of the Mexican population of Northwestern New Mexico, the industry of the inhabitants being limited to agriculture and pastoral pursuits. In this section are in-

cluded five Mexican plazas, clustered together along the Rio Chama and its tributaries.

Las Nutritas [now Tierra Amarilla] is the largest of the group, to which sometimes the name of the section itself is applied. It derives its name from the creek upon whose banks it lies, a tributary of the Chama. The name *La Nutrita*, a diminutive, signifies "the little otter." By a provincialism, however, they employ *nutria* as a beaver, using to designate an otter the expression *perro del agua* or waterdog. The town is equidistant from Los Ojos and Encinada, two miles from each. It contains three stores — that of Burns, an American, annual sales of $20,000; Johnson & Co., $8,000 to $10,000; and Th. Escabal, $5,000 — a shoe-shop, and blacksmith building. The post-office of the section was located here, mails being weekly only and from no direction save from Santa Fe to the south; population, 250.

Los Ojos (The Springs) is on the Rio Chama, due west from Las Nutritas 2 miles. It contains 4 stores, one a branch of Burns' at Nutritas, annual sales given as $10,000, and three Mexican, small affairs, sales aggregating perhaps $8,000. It is 1-½ miles below Los Brazos, and its population is 180. The Chama River is forded at this point for all directions west, its altitude being 7,300 feet, while that of Las Nutritas is 7,480.

La Puente (The Bridge) is on the Chama, 2 miles from Las Nutritas and some distance southeast from Los Ojos; no stores; a small plaza; population, 100.

Encinada (The Oak) is 2 miles above Las Nutritas, on the East Fork of the Chama, sometimes called Rio Brazos, and same distance east of Los Ojos. There are no stores here; it is a second-rate plaza of 100.

Los Brazos (The Arms), from its location at the junction of the two main forks in the river, at an altitude of 7,350 feet. It is 1-½ miles north of Los Ojos, and, like it, is on the river-bank. There are no stores here, and in population it numbers 170.

The entire population of the Tierra Amarilla section is 800.[14]

McCauley's population estimates are generally confirmed by the 1880 census except that Los Ojos then had 346 residents and the total population of the villages was 923.

Two events in the early 1880s marked a turning point in the development of the region. The effects of the first, the arrival of the railroad in 1880, were quickly felt;

—

9. Los Ojos (Burns Stores/Tierra Wools left) about 1890. Photo courtesy Museum of New Mexico.

the effects of the second, the final confirmation of the Tierra Amarilla Grant in 1883, took seventy-five years to be fully felt. The Denver and Rio Grande Railway dipped south into New Mexico and the Chama valley before heading north again for Durango, Colorado, and the San Juan gold and silver district. A railroad service center named Chama was established ten miles to the north of the original Spanish villages. It represented the first permanent Anglo-American settlement in the area and brought the valley more directly into the national mercantile economy. Coffee and sugar, cast iron stoves and calico, steel plows and barbed wire all became more readily available. For architecture, the most important imports were carpentry tools, finished doors and windows, roofing shingles and wooden ornament. In exchange for these manufactured items, the valley began to produce goods for export, chiefly lumber and wool.

Meanwhile, the Tierra Amarilla Grant, which Congress had confirmed in 1860, needed a detailed land survey before the final confirmation, known as a patent, could be issued. Despite the lack of surveyed boundaries, T.D. Burns nevertheless began purchasing deeds to the grant from descendants of Manuel Martinez about

10. Jose R. Martinez Store and House, Tierra Amarilla about 1890. Photo by Otto Preusse, courtesy Museum of New Mexico.

1865. In 1874, Thomas Catron, prominent Santa Fe lawyer and later U.S. Senator, joined the speculation in deeds, and by 1880 Catron could lay claim to all of the grant except the small farm plots belonging to the original settlers.

Catron's control hinged on two legal issues. The first issue was whether the grant had been a community grant to the entire group of settlers or a private grant made solely to Manuel Martinez and his family. Typically in the Spanish/Mexican tradition, the only name that appears in documents is that of the leader and spokesman of the group of settlers. The general term for this person was *poblador principal;* although local tradition recognizes Martinez with the term *el Mercenado.* Scholars generally agree today that a series of Mexican documents indicate that this was a community grant. But in 1860, through mistranslation of one document and suppression of another, Congress was lead to confirm the Tierra Amarilla grant as a private grant. The phrase *me quieren acompañar,* in Martinez's request for the grant, was incorrectly translated into the subjunctive as "Manuel Martinez together with eight male children and others *who may voluntarily desire to accompany him.*" The correct translation, "others *who desire to accompany me,*" as land grant historian Malcomb Ebright has pointed out, gives a clear indication of a group of settlers ready to occupy the grant, a group of which Martinez was the leader.[16]

By the time the grant was confirmed by Congress, Manuel had died, and his son Francisco set about issuing deeds to the other settlers. Between 1860 and 1865 Francisco deeded them individual fields and added that "the said *varas* [fields] retain the right of pastures, water, firewood, timbers and roads, free and common." The second legal issue turned on this passage. Although it had been confirmed as a private grant and heirs of Manuel Martinez would soon begin selling their share of the grant to land speculators, Francisco Martinez nevertheless appears to have deeded traditional use of the common lands to the others as though it were a community grant. When Catron filed a quiet title suit in 1883 to consolidate his claim to the grant, however, these rights to common lands were ignored. He excluded the villages and irrigated fields from the land he was claiming. This allowed the villagers, who had a possible claim to the property in question, to be omitted from the list of those who would have to receive written notice of the proceedings. The court ignored the possible claims of the villagers even though more than one hundred of them had registered their deeds from Martinez at the county courthouse.

When their claims to the common lands were pursued in court in the 1950s (after the last of the commons were fenced), they were disallowed on two grounds: first, that because Congress had confirmed the grant as an individual grant, the question could not be raised in court and second, that the deeds from Francisco Martinez to the settlers, which gave them a renewed claim to the commons, had been improperly worded. The deeds used the verb *quedar* (to retain), which does not have the same legal force as "I give" or "I grant," which is the wording required under English common law for a transfer of property.[17] There is now general agreement among those who have studied and written on the history of this grant that the settlers' loss of common lands was unjust, whether one attributes the loss to unfortunate differences between the property laws of the United States and Mexico or to outright legislative and judicial chicanery.[18]

In 1880, three years before the completion of his quiet title suit, Catron sold portions of the grant to the Denver and Rio Grande Railway for construction of their rail lines and for the Chama depot and shops site. Commercial logging of the common lands, which commenced at the same time to supply the railroad with ties and bridge timbers, continued into the twentieth century. In 1912, the northern portions of the grant began to be fenced by an outside cattle company. Fencing by private owners progressed steadily between the World Wars.

From the earliest years of settlement, the subsistence agriculture of the area had been inadequate to supply all the needs of the villagers. Because of the high altitude and short growing season, many fruits and vegetables could not be grown. To supplement local produce, trade was conducted with lower-lying villages. Some men in

—

11. Tierra Amarilla (Courthouse right), early 1920s. Photo courtesy Erlinda Luna.

the new villages also continued a tradition of buffalo hunting that had been practiced by Abiquiu residents. From Tierra Amarilla, the hunters, known as *ciboleros*,
made the long journey east through the mountains and the San Luis Valley of Colorado to the Great Plains. For two decades, until about 1880 when the buffalo were
decimated, these *ciboleros* returned from their annual expeditions with loads of buffalo robes and dried meat.

Just as the *cibolero* tradition was passing, it was replaced by the availability of
wage work in the construction and later the operation of the railroad and in logging
and lumber mills. Men moved temporarily to jobs in Chama or the logging camps,
but their wives and children remained in the villages. The E.M. Biggs sawmill was
established in 1888 at Chama, and in 1896 a rail line was extended twelve miles
south to Tierra Amarilla and another ten miles southeast along Nutritas Creek to
reach stands of timber. In 1902, after the area had been logged out, the line was
dismantled and the materials were reused in the construction of a new lumber
railroad south from Lumberton to El Vado, twelve miles southwest of Tierra
Amarilla. Local men helped to build this line and subsequently worked in the
sawmill at El Vado.[19]

By 1928, the timber near Lumberton and El Vado also was exhausted, and the operation was moved again, north and west to Dolores, Colorado. While the timberlands were being exhausted and the pastures were being fenced by outside ranchers, the local fields were also becoming smaller as they were subdivided through inheritance. This declining economic basis, combined with the increasing population of the villages, led local men to seek work farther from home in mining, construction and agriculture. During Prohibition, which began in nearby Colorado in 1916, some took up bootlegging.[20]

The advent of state and federal public works projects during the 1930s provided new jobs locally, especially in the construction of highways and of the El Vado Dam. Nevertheless, a project such as the construction of the state fish hatchery south of Los Ojos from 1932 to 1934 was viewed with ambivalence locally. While such projects did provide jobs, they also represented the government's development of the once communally used mountains as a recreational area for outsiders. The widened horizons of the young men who returned from the two World Wars, combined with the shortage of local jobs, stimulated emigration to Española, Santa Fe and Albuquerque, Pueblo, Denver and beyond.

12. Tierra Amarilla (just north of Courthouse), about 1945. Photo courtesy Fr. Austin Ernstes.

The struggle to maintain the traditional economy suffered a set back when the last common lands were fenced by cattle companies in the early 1950s. Long-festering resentments throughout northern New Mexico about the loss of communal lands surfaced in a movement to regain control of the land grants led by Reies Lopez Tijerina. This movement culminated in 1967 with a declaration of independence from the United States and a raid on the Rio Arriba county courthouse at Tierra Amarilla. Outside attention was focused on the area, causing an increase in federal social programs and leading to scholarly examination of the history of the land grant.[21]

Current initiatives to revitalize the local culture and economy through a community medical clinic, a weavers' cooperative and a sheepherders' cooperative stem from this period of activism. Other area residents work as teachers, as Forest Service employees or in the county courthouse. Seasonal work is available repairing highways ravaged by the hard winters and in the summer tourist businesses in Chama. Some households receive retirement or public assistance benefits. Many families also keep the agricultural traditions alive with their few head of livestock, sustained by home-grown alfalfa and, perhaps, a few Forest Service grazing permits.[22]

13. Los Ojos at Hatchery turn off, about 1945. Photo courtesy New Mexico Tourism & Travel.

2 — Architecture

Pioneers who moved outward in all directions from the core of Hispanic settlement along the upper Rio Grande, beginning about 1790, carried a shared architectural tradition. The buildings that they constructed, which remain standing by the thousands in New Mexico and southern Colorado, share a basic plan and a common set of materials and construction techniques. A number of local variations of this tradition developed, however, in response to differing climatic conditions, locally available materials, and proximity to the railroad and to neighboring cultures. Mountains that isolate one valley from another encouraged this local variation. Perhaps the most distinctive local style developed in the six villages of the Tierra Amarilla area.

Here, as elsewhere in Hispanic New Mexico, houses have single-file plans, adobe or log walls and corrugated metal roofs. In Tierra Amarilla, however, the roof is often raised on a tall parapet wall to create a second-story space used for bedrooms as well as for storage. These story-and-a-half houses frequently have dormers, gable balconies, and porches lining two and sometimes three sides of the building. Pitched roofs, dormers and second stories introduced by Anglo-Americans were integrated by Hispanic builders into their flat-roofed building tradition. In La Tierra Amarilla by the 1880s, a local, hybrid architectural type developed. This style predominated

14. Fernando Martinez Store/House, Los Brazos, built 1910.

15

15. Jacal Construction, Ulibarri Shed, La Puente.

through the Second World War and continues to influence some building today. This local architecture is utterly unique and constitutes a vivid, well-preserved example of how one cultural tradition adopts and adapts elements of another culture.

The earliest buildings of both the temporary summer camps and the permanent villages of 1860 and 1861 were probably constructed of logs, the most convenient and abundant material. The simplest form of log construction, known as *jacal*, consists of logs, five to eight inches in diameter, placed on end side-by-side in a trench. The trimmed, wedge-shaped tops of the logs are fitted into a grooved cross beam. *Jacal* was used to build houses at least until 1915 and for outbuildings until 1940.

All horizontal log buildings are known locally as *fuertes*, a term originally meaning fort or stronghold and used elsewhere in New Mexico for a building that can be locked and used to store saddles, harnesses and tools. The typical Hispanic form of horizontal log construction employs double box-notching and logs that have been hewn flat with an ax on the outside and inside surfaces. This was the first log construction technique used in the Tierra Amarilla area, and it remained important until about 1910.[1]

Many *fuertes* reused logs from Fort Lowell. The fort was manned and the first buildings were erected in 1866 by a company of New Mexico volunteers. Being Hispanic, they likely built with hewn logs and double box-notching. These volunteers were replaced during the second year of the fort's operation by a unit of the U.S. Thirty-Third Infantry formed in Arkansas. This regular Army unit constructed additional log structures. In Arkansas, construction with unhewn, round logs, double saddle-notching and to a lesser extent dovetail notching was popular, and these techniques were likely used for the buildings constructed during the second year. The double saddle-notch form was subsequently employed for about

16. Upper left, double box notching, Francisco Luna Barn, Tierra Amarilla.

17. Above, double saddle notching, barn, Los Ojos. Photo by Robert Torrez.

18. Left, half dovetail notching (with some earthen plaster), house, La Puente.

19. Railroad tie construction, Abeyta Garage, Los Brazos.

one-third of the local log structures, mostly for small barns, sheds and storage cellars. There are a few local examples of dovetail and half-dovetail notching, which were not normally employed in Hispanic New Mexico; these may have been introduced by soldiers at Fort Lowell or by the Swedish settlers of the original Park View.

The predominant form of construction in Abiquiu, from which the first settlers of La Tierra Amarilla came, was adobe, and these settlers showed a preference for adobe over log construction in their new villages. The Spanish, who learned adobe brick making from the Arabs, had introduced the technique to New Mexico. The Pueblo Indians built of earth prior to the arrival of the Spanish, but they used hand-formed courses called puddled adobe, not adobe bricks. Adobes are made by placing moistened earth into a wooden mold. Straw is often added to the mixture to facilitate even drying by wicking moisture to the outside of the brick. If the mixture is dry enough, just about the stiffness of tortilla dough, the form can be removed quickly, and after about two days the bricks can be stood on end to dry. After another week, the adobes are stacked for a month of sun drying.

Historically, adobes were laid with an earthen mortar, sometimes beginning directly on the ground. Often, though, a foundation was formed by digging a trench a foot or so deep and the width of the wall and filling this trench with field stone. The concrete copings around the bases of many area houses were poured in place in recent years to protect the outside edge of the walls from erosion by ground moisture.[2]

———

Large timbers became harder to find as the villages became settled and individual families prospered, and adobe emerged as the primary building material. The first room of many houses is *jacal* or *fuerte* with later additions constructed of adobe. Sometimes, though, a separate, new adobe house was built, and the original cabin was converted into a storage building or incorporated into a barn. While logs were used for both houses and barns, adobe was rarely used for outbuildings or barns; today the Luna Barn in Tierra Amarilla is the only remaining adobe barn.

About 1900, horizontal log construction began to be replaced by two forms of construction using milled lumber. One is box construction, in which walls are formed by sets of planks placed side-by-side and joined by crossing boards at both ends. Although Anglo-American box construction generally runs the planks vertically (and frequently covers the joints between boards with thin battens), in La Tierra Amarilla planks are usually run horizontally, perhaps echoing the tradition of horizontal log construction. The relation to horizontal log construction is even

20. Jacal room (lower left), adobe addition (right), vertical planks with lath and earthen plaster (above), Ortiz House, Los Ojos.

clearer in the other lumber building technique, which consists of railroad ties laid horizontally. Both forms of construction were used for farm buildings and houses, but outbuildings went unsurfaced while houses always received wood lath and earthen stucco on the outside and lath and hard plaster inside.

The New Mexican Hispanic building tradition was modular, with the individual room forming the basic unit and houses growing gradually, a room or two at a time.[3] A family generally began by building a single, self-sufficient room, usually rectangular in shape, with a single door on one of the long sides. Research on Hispanic houses elsewhere in New Mexico suggests that in the mid-nineteenth century, even in large houses, a single room often served as the focus of all household activities: sleeping and cooking, eating, bathing and entertaining.[4] As the growth of the family required, and resources allowed, additional rooms were added.

Each room was essentially like the first, a separate module with its own exterior door. The original, one-room, log portions are clearly visible in some deteriorating Tierra Amarilla houses. In better-maintained houses, plaster conceals the underlying material, whether adobe or log or a combination of the two. The change of materials from one room to the next is one sign of the modular tradition. Another indication of this tradition is the frequent occurrence of steps between rooms, a result of rooms being built directly on the ground, where they follow the slope of the building site.

Interior doors between rooms were sometimes omitted; movement from room to room often occurred, instead, outside the house. The narrow porches frequently added after 1880 sheltered this exterior circulation. Interior doors between rooms were added in some houses as late as the 1950s.

Many one- and two-room houses still stand, although none are occupied. Most houses are three or four rooms arranged in a single file. If more rooms were added, a corner was usually turned to form an L-shaped, or possibly a U-shaped house. The presence of more than five rooms (and doors) frequently indicates a row of two or more connected houses, which were originally occupied by related families. Underlying this additive process was the Spanish ideal of the courtyard house with fifteen or so rooms enclosing a patio. Some full courtyard houses were built in the Hispanic homeland along the upper Rio Grande. No Tierra Amarilla houses achieved this form, however, in part because the development of second-story living space redirected later additions upward.

Shortly after the American occupation of 1846, the first sawmills were established in New Mexico, and with the arrival of the railroad in 1880, milled lumber and wooden roofing shingles became widely available. These materials and an influx of Anglo-American carpenters led to the addition of pitched roofs on existing structures and to the incorporation of the gabled roof form into the Hispanic building

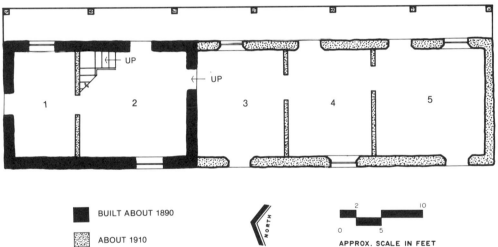

BUILT ABOUT 1890

ABOUT 1910

NORTH

APPROX. SCALE IN FEET

21/22. Rascon House (rear view), Los Ojos, built beginning about 1890.

tradition. The vast majority of Hispanic houses, particularly north of Albuquerque, now have pitched roofs. The storage attics that these roofs create, like the rooms below, are conceived of as discrete units with their own exterior, gable-end doors reached by ladders. The attics of many Tierra Amarilla houses are used in this manner only for storage and food drying.

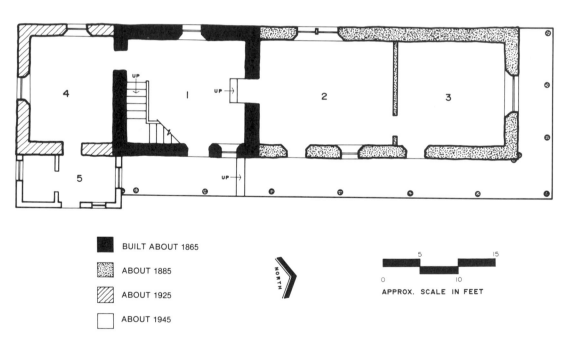

BUILT ABOUT 1865

ABOUT 1885

ABOUT 1925

ABOUT 1945

NORTH

5   15

0   10

APPROX. SCALE IN FEET

23/24. Valdez House, Los Ojos, built beginning about 1865.

These then were the norms of the New Mexican Hispanic building tradition during the late nineteenth and early twentieth centuries: adobe or heavy timber construction, single file plans with multiple exterior doors, and steeply pitched roofs over storage attics.[5] A good example of these characteristics is the Rascon House, which stood in Los Ojos until it was demolished about 1985. It began in the late nineteenth century as a *fuerte* — a one-room, flat-roofed, hewn-log house. A three-room addition built early this century consisted of horizontal planks covered with lath and earthen plaster. The addition was leveled on a partial stone foundation, but its floor stood seven inches lower than that of the original cabin. The pitched roof, with two dormers on the front side, was added at the same time as the three-room addition, along with the interior stairs and a partition dividing the original cabin into two rooms. Multiroom additions and the partitioning of existing large rooms often indicate the development of specialized rooms — a kitchen and a parlor, bedrooms and storage.

The Valdez House is a more elaborate example of the local type. The continuous slope of the roof over the porch disguises the story-and-a-half construction. Like the previous example, this house was built in stages. The original flat-roofed, one-room house was constructed about 1865. The two rooms added twenty years later stand fourteen inches higher than the original portion, necessitating steps between rooms and on the porch. The unifying porch and gable roof, which created second-story bedrooms and storage, was also added about 1885. In this century, the new, shed-roofed kitchen and finally a small bathroom were added. Although the narrow porch serves as an exterior corridor, the primary movement on the ground floor is inside from room to room.

The first pitched roofs in the area were built at Camp Plummer (later called Fort Lowell), which was active from 1865 to 1869.[6] An historical bird's eye view and a plan of the camp show the officers' quarters consisting of four separate units each composed of sixteen-foot-square modules. The five-room commander's quarters (second from the right) had a centered door flanked by symmetrically placed windows. The front entrance opened onto a slightly-narrower-than-normal room, which served as a sort of corridor to the rooms on either side. In the three-room, junior officers' quarters, the front door opened onto a similar public room, which probably served as a living room and led to a bedroom to the side and to what may have been a kitchen at the rear.

Five Tierra Amarilla houses combine features from the commander's quarters and the smaller, junior officers' quarters to form a distinctive local house type. One example, situated close to the fort site, is commonly referred to as the Officer's House (illustration 97). A second example, the Sanchez House, which lies two miles north

—

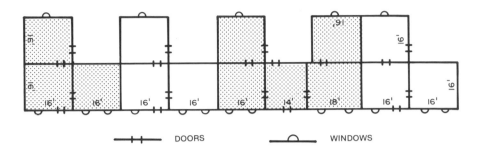

9'

16' 16' 16' 16' 16' 14 18' 16' 9' 16' 16'

├─┤┼─┤ DOORS   ╭─╮ WINDOWS

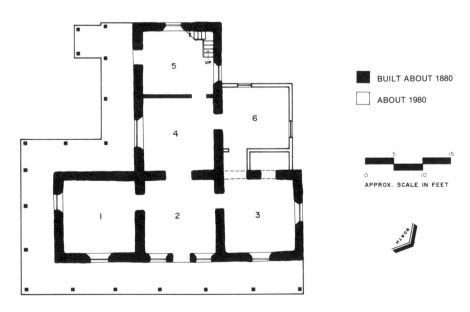

5   UP

6

4

1   2   3

■ BUILT ABOUT 1880

□ ABOUT 1980

5   15
0   10
APPROX. SCALE IN FEET

NORTH

24

on the road between Los Ojos and Los Brazos, was built about 1880 of adobe, using a five-room T-shaped plan. Its distinctive facade symmetry, with a window on either side of a tight window/door/window group, which is characteristic of this local Officer's House type, is adapted from the commander's unit.

In terms of circulation (that is, the paths of movement within the house), the Officer's House is a translation of the popular Anglo-American center hall house plan (like the Jose R. Martinez House discussed later) into the sixteen-foot-square modules of the log fort and of the local Hispanic tradition. The front door opens into a living room, which doubles as a corridor to the dining room and kitchen at the rear and to the bedrooms to the sides. The stairs in the kitchen lead to second floor bedrooms and storage. This floor plan begins with the L-shaped junior officers' quarters, adds another room to the side of the entry room, like the commander's quarters, and places an extra room to the rear, perhaps reflecting the Hispanic linear tradition. (A bathroom and closets were added within the last ten years.)

Camp Plummer and the subsequent Officer's House type introduced pitched roofs, facade symmetry and the separation of public and private space into individual rooms. Military post construction had a similar impact on local architecture throughout the Southwest.

The arrival of the railroad in 1880 greatly affected both the economy and the architecture of Tierra Amarilla. While no builders or carpenters are listed on the 1870 census enumerator sheets, fourteen carpenters, three masons and a bricklayer appear in 1880, twelve with Hispanic surnames and six with non-Hispanic names. A handful of local houses adopted Anglo-American house plans outright. The first of these plans was a two-story, hipped-roof type with a centered entrance and centered halls on both floors. The origin of this symmetrical plan can be traced back through the Greek Revival, which was popular in the East in the 1830s and 1840s, to the Georgian House of English Colonial days. Six of these were built in the mid-1880s for wealthy Hispanic livestock owners and merchants. The Jose R. Martinez House in Tierra Amarilla, with its elaborately detailed porches, is a particularly good example of the type. Interestingly, a subsequent addition to this structure follows the Hispanic linear tradition.

Another locally adapted Anglo-American house plan was the one-story Hipped Cottage. The best example of this type, the Lopez House in Los Ojos, has symmetrically placed windows, doors and rooms like the two-story mansions. But its

25. Above left, detail of "Camp Plummer, New Mexico, December 31st, 1867," by D. Mortimer Lee, showing the Officers' Quarters. Redrawn from the original in the National Archives. Every other unit shaded.

26/27. Middle and bottom left, Sanchez-March House, north of Los Ojos, built about 1880.

28/29. Jose R. Martinez House, Tierra Amarilla, built about 1885. Photo by E.A. Wilder, courtesy Museum of New Mexico.

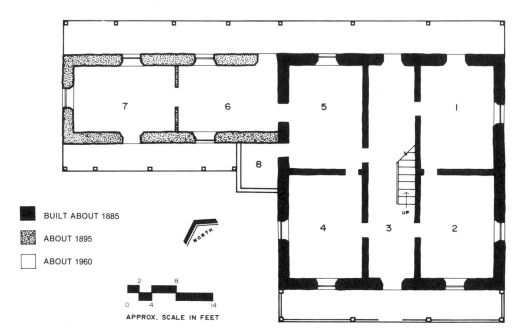

BUILT ABOUT 1885
ABOUT 1895
ABOUT 1960

NORTH

APPROX. SCALE IN FEET

30. Above right, Lopez-Martinez House, Los Ojos, built about 1895.

31. Middle right, Esquibel House, Tierra Amarilla, built about 1900.

32. Bottom right, Antonio Lente House, Los Ojos, built about 1900.

centered hall extends only halfway into the house: at the front of the house, the hall is flanked on either side by a pair of rooms, but this hall opens directly into the middle of the three rooms at the back. These two house types introduced the hipped roof and center halls, and they reinforced other design elements already suggested by the Officer's House type.

Most Hispanic builders adopted one or two isolated elements — the hipped roof, facade symmetry or a full second story — but retained the basic tradition of linear accretion. The builder of the Frank Esquibel House in Tierra Amarilla, for instance, continued the tradition of an exterior door for each room but arranged the doors at the front symmetrically. This builder also combined a hipped roof with the story-and-a-half form normally used only with linear houses.

Another approach to the combination of a second story with the Hispanic linear tradition was taken by the builder of the Lente House in Los Ojos. In a sense, it is a traditional, six room, U-shaped house, split in half and stacked. By wrapping the porch around the L-shaped plan, the builder maintained access to each room's exterior door. Although this is an efficient solution, only three local houses combine a full two-story porch with a linear plan, and the four-square Esquibel house is unlike any other remaining local house.

The more typical two-story houses in the area use the story-and-a-half form with gable and wall dormers, which place the lower half of the window in the wall and the upper half of the dormer above the roof eaves (illustration 85). A similar story-and-a-half form with gable and wall dormers was common to Gothic Revival style houses built across the country from the 1840s to the 1880s.[7] Relatively few examples, which potentially could have introduced the form to Tierra Amarilla builders, were constructed in New Mexico, however, and none remain in Chama, the closest Anglo-American settlement. Drawings of Gothic Revival cottages did appear in house pattern books that may have been seen by local builders.

Only two other concentrations of story-and-a-half houses exist in the Hispanic core of northern New Mexico and southern Colorado: one in Wagon Mound, New Mexico, the other in the villages of the San Luis Valley of Colorado. Both of these areas lack the gable balconies and elaborate porches of Tierra Amarilla. While Wagon Mound is over one hundred miles to the east and beyond two mountain ranges, contact between La Tierra Amarilla and the San Luis Valley, fifty miles to the northeast, has been common since the 1860s.[8] The story-and-a-half form appears to have been introduced to the San Luis Valley by Mormon settlers; an enclave of Mormon villages — Richfield, Sanford and Manassa — were established there beginning in 1878.[9]

33. Mormon House, Richfield, Colorado, built about 1885.

34. Vigil-Chavez House, San Pedro, Colorado, built about 1890.

35. Ramon Jaramillo house, Ensenada, built in 1887.

By the early 1880s, a number of symmetrical story-and-a-half houses had been constructed in these new Mormon communities, houses similar to those of the Sanpete Valley around Manti, Utah, from which many of the settlers had come. These houses frequently have a center hall plan and, on the exterior, a centered gable dormer with a door that opens onto a balcony over the entrance porch. These gable dormers are also often flanked by wall dormers.[10] The Vigil-Chavez residence in San Pedro, Colorado, began as a flat-roofed, linear, three-room house but was later expanded under the influence of the Mormon houses. The builder reconciled the Hispanic requirement for an exterior door to each room with the Mormon-introduced facade symmetry by providing a door to the front off the middle room and a pair of symmetrically placed doors to the rear off the side rooms.

36. House, Ensenada, built about 1900.

37. Valdez House, Los Brazos, built about 1895.

38. Fernando Salazar House, Los Ojos, built about 1900, two interior stairs.

There is some historical documentation suggesting direct contact between La Tierra Amarilla and the Mormon communities, but Mormon architectural ideas may well have been passed through the intermediate Hispanic villages of the San Luis Valley.[11] Tierra Amarilla builders adopted the story-and-a-half form and either wall or gable dormers, but not both dormer types in any one house. In contrast to the symmetrical facades of the Mormon type, the dormers and multiple doors of Tierra Amarilla houses are located informally, in relation to interior spaces rather than for exterior formality. In addition to architectural features, Mormon hay derricks were also adopted in the Tierra Amarilla area.[12] Hispanic-Mormon contact seems apparent from these material culture features and logical given the proximity of the two groups. Indeed, cultural influence moved in the opposite direction as well: Mormons learned to make adobes, which they called Spanish bricks, from Hispanics. And, in the San Luis Valley, Hispanic villagers provided food and shelter to help sustain the Mormons through their first winter.[13]

The balconies of Tierra Amarilla houses are located on gable ends, unlike the facade balconies of Mormon houses or the balconies of the local two-story, center-hall houses. The gable location of the balconies continues the traditional linear axis of expansion. It is an easy progression from a ladder reaching a gable door to permanent exterior stairs, and from that to the extension of the gabled roof over the stairway, and finally to a full balcony.

The Fernando Martinez House in Los Brazos is one of the largest, most elaborate examples of the distinctive Tierra Amarilla house type and of the gradual growth of a house along with a family. According to family tradition, the original three-room, flat-roofed adobe house was built in 1868. Fernando married Soledad in 1876, and as children began to arrive in the 1880s, the house was expanded by a fourth room on the ground floor and a pitched roof, which created three additional rooms above. (The thick *jacal* wall between rooms four and five — the only nonadobe wall — may have been reused from an earlier building.) The family grew to eight children, and in 1910, Fernando built the large building (illustration 14) thirty feet to the south, which housed a grocery on the ground floor and a three-room residence above. In 1912, the family built the large wing on the north of the original house for the oldest son, Pedro. Another son, Jose Espiridion, first inherited the store, which later passed to Fernando junior. After Fernando's death in 1914, Soledad remained with the younger children in rooms one and two of the original house and those above — rooms ten and eleven. Two of the sons formed two-room households with a kitchen/parlor on the ground floor and a bedroom above: Jose del Carmen in rooms three and twelve and Onecimo in rooms four and thirteen. Like many area houses, the first bathroom was added to the rear (the small room between rooms 8 and 9) in the 1920s or 1930s.[14]

By the mid 1940s, the house was compartmentalized into three households with separate owners, and the doors were blocked between rooms two and three and between four and five. Over a number of years, Medardo Sanchez and his wife Clorinda, a granddaughter of Fernando senior, purchased the separate sections from relatives, and in 1986 they converted the house into a bed and breakfast inn. The second floor was divided into seven bedrooms, two baths and a sitting room, although the plan included here shows the second floor before this remodeling.

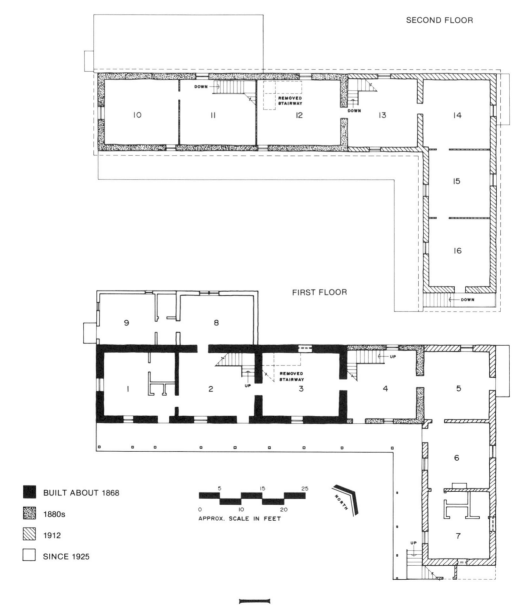

SECOND FLOOR

10   11   12   REMOVED STAIRWAY   DOWN   13   14

15

16

FIRST FLOOR

9   8

1   2   REMOVED STAIRWAY   3   4   5

6

7

BUILT ABOUT 1868

1880s

1912

SINCE 1925

APPROX. SCALE IN FEET

NORTH

The pattern of linear additions seen in area houses also shaped outbuildings and barns. The basic, modular unit for service buildings is the rectangular log crib, generally with a door and sometimes a window in one long side. Additional units (sometimes with a different log-notching style) were added in linear fashion but at a distance from the first section. The span between the units was then bridged by log cross beams, and the rear wall was completed with *jacal* or vertical wood planks. These barns were originally flatroofed and piled high in the fall with hay. Most barns were subsequently given pitched roofs, and many of these employed plank walls to raise the gable roof like the half-story wall of local houses. A dormer door or a simple break in this plank wall allowed access to the hay loft. Occasionally,

42. Miguel Valdez Barn, Ensenada, perhaps built about 1920.

43. Barn, Los Ojos, built about 1890.

39/40/41. Left, Fernando Martinez House, Los Brazos, built beginning in 1868.

shed-roofed rooms were added at the ends of these barns, and a variety of small sheds and outbuildings complemented the barn. Starting in the 1920s, double doors were cut into the short end of some outbuildings to form garages, and a few freestanding garages were constructed, frequently of railroad ties.

In the Spanish tradition, residences and outbuildings were often arranged into a single rectangular courtyard unit known as a *casa corral*.[15] The residence generally stood at the front along the street's edge, with the farm buildings to the rear and, if necessary, an adobe wall completing the enclosed compound. A few larger examples, in older communities such as Santa Fe and Taos, had a full residential courtyard with an attached corral courtyard to the rear. This tradition underlies the placing of many Tierra Amarilla buildings, such as the house and barn complex built by Gumercindo Salazar in La Puente during the 1890s (see also illustration 8, left). The house (# 1 on the plan) was destroyed by a fire in the early 1980s. It stood at the front of the complex, but with a porch facing the street and a fenced front yard in the Anglo-American style. The large barn (# 6), hog pens (# 5), a chicken coop (# 4), a portion of the neighbor's *jacal* and horizontal log outbuilding(# 10) and a six-foot-high plank fence complete the corral compound. One of the barn's log cribs stored tools and farm implements; the other, which is earthen plastered, probably was used to store grain. The middle section of the barn formed a stable for Salazar's team of horses, and the hay loft ran above all three sections. In addition to the work horses, hogs and chickens, sheep were occasionally kept in the compound at shearing time. A three-foot-tall wire fence separates the corral from a domestic work space along the rear of the house. There, in easy proximity, are the well (# 2) located in the original kitchen; the *horno* (# 9), an oven used for baking bread and drying food; a log room with an excavated storage cellar (# 3); and a garden plot (# 11).

44. Horno (oven), Gumercindo Salazar Casa Corral Complex, La Puente.

45. Gumercindo Salazar Barn, La Puente, built 1897-98.

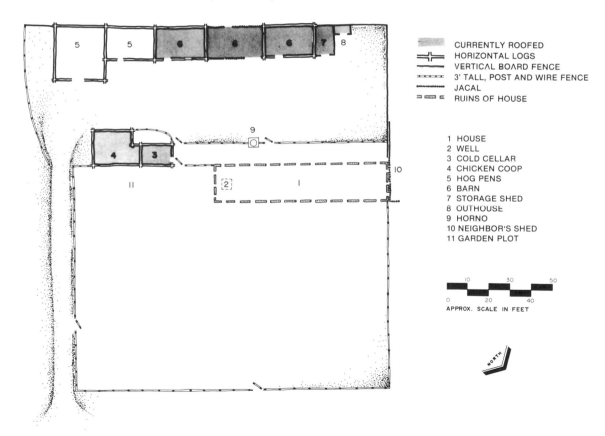

CURRENTLY ROOFED
HORIZONTAL LOGS
VERTICAL BOARD FENCE
3' TALL, POST AND WIRE FENCE
JACAL
RUINS OF HOUSE

1 HOUSE
2 WELL
3 COLD CELLAR
4 CHICKEN COOP
5 HOG PENS
6 BARN
7 STORAGE SHED
8 OUTHOUSE
9 HORNO
10 NEIGHBOR'S SHED
11 GARDEN PLOT

10   30   50
0   20   40
APPROX. SCALE IN FEET

NORTH

46. Gumercindo Salazar House-Barn-Corral Complex, La Puente.

47. Left, porch detail, Jose R. Martinez Building, Tierra Amarilla, built about 1885.

48. Left bottom, porch detail, Archuleta House, Los Ojos, built about 1890.

49. Right bottom, porch detail, Fernando Martinez Store-House, Los Brazos, built 1910.

The influence of national architectural styles is limited in most houses to wood ornament concentrated around doors and windows and on porches and balconies. The influence of the Greek Revival or, as it is called in New Mexico, the Territorial style can be seen in the pedimented lintels and chamfered porch posts with molding "capitals" found on the finer houses dating to the 1870s and early 1880s. A few local carpenters also crafted their own jigsawn ornament, but most porches and balconies use stock details purchased from the lumberyard. Queen Anne style details — slender, lathe-turned columns and cut-out brackets — were available in the railroad town of Chama from 1880 until about 1905; at the turn of the century, stouter classical columns also became available. Many simpler houses were built with unadorned, chamfered posts produced at the local lumbermill.

Windows were also a lumberyard stock item, one that periodically changed in design; as a result, window types can help to date a building. In general, double-hung sash windows with two, vertical panes over two similar panes date to 1875-1900 (illustration 30); one-over-one double hung windows date to 1880-1900 (illustration 23); four-over-four windows to 1900-1935 (illustration 89); and four pane wood casement or sliding windows to 1920-1940 (illustration 105).

About twenty of the most prominent houses in La Tierra Amarilla have brick chimneys that step out near their tops to form cornices. These chimneys are actually made of brick only on the exterior where they are exposed to the elements; just below the roof, adobe flues lead down to fireplaces; or, more often, to cast iron stoves.

50. San Joaquin Church, Ensenada, built 1915.

51. Parkview Super Market, Los Ojos, built about 1890, facade about 1910.

Specialized buildings, although few in number, are of pivotal importance in the communities. Catholic churches were given the most prominent locations at the intersection of roads or facing onto informal plazas, underscoring their importance in the community. San Joaquin church in Ensenada and San Miguel church in La Puente are like many New Mexican village chapels in their nearly domestic scale and use of standard materials — adobe, stock windows and intersecting, corrugated metal roofs. The main parish churches for the area, San Jose at Los Ojos and Santo Niño in Tierra Amarilla, are larger structures with pointed, Gothic Revival windows and attached rectories for the resident priests.

School houses built around the turn of the century remain in Los Ojos, Los Brazos and Plaza Blanca. They are long, narrow, adobe buildings with corrugated metal roofs. Only the location of a door and porch on the short, gable end, and the presence of a small belfry make them quickly distinguishable from houses. Their basic domestic appearance is underscored by the fact that the first school in Los Ojos was easily converted into a house about 1930. The Plaza Blanca school has been converted into a chapel, while the Los Brazos school stands empty and deteriorating. The Rio Arriba County Courthouse, designed in 1916 by Santa Fe architects Rapp, Rapp and Hendrickson in the Neo-classical style, is a striking departure from the local building tradition.

Most of the commercial buildings, too, have a basically domestic scale; they are distinguished chiefly by display windows flanking a centered entrance, usually located on the gable end. Only in Los Ojos and Tierra Amarilla, the leading mercantile centers, were the traditional domestic forms pushed to a larger scale and given distinctive detailing. The T.D. Burns store in Los Ojos has a brick veneer facade (illustration 77), and the Park View Market has a faintly classical, pressed metal cornice. The Burns store in Tierra Amarilla (destroyed in the 1970s) had a prominent California Mission style porch (illustration 80). Service stations and shops catering to the increasing auto traffic were built along (Old) Highway 84 in Tierra Amarilla and Los Ojos during the late 1920s and the 1930s. Generally constructed of hollow tile or railroad ties, these buildings have stepping profiles along the tops of their parapet walls, which evoke the Mission style and the Spanish Pueblo Revival style. Lito's Ballroom in Tierra Amarilla is the most distinctive of these highway era buildings.

52. Archuleta Store, Tierra Amarilla, built about 1885.

53. Lito's Ballroom, Tierra Amarilla, built about 1925.

The architecture of La Tierra Amarilla suggests significant acculturation after 1870, brought about by Camp Plummer, by the railroad and itinerant carpenters and, probably, by Mormon influences transmitted through the Hispanic villages of the San Luis Valley. In the late 1800s, Hispanic New Mexicans found themselves cut off from Spain and Mexico; they were surrounded and their culture and institutions were under increasing pressure from the dominant Anglo-American culture. In architecture, their previously flat-roofed tradition with its multiple doors and linear plans did not square easily with Anglo-American introductions such as facade symmetry, pitched roofs and second stories. The ingenious ways that Tierra Amarilla builders found to incorporate these new ideas into the informal, additive Spanish tradition produced a truly distinctive architecture.

3 — Land and Water Use

"La Tierra es nuestra madre," states one farmer.
"The land and our water system have always been the livelihood of
the people," states another.

Such sentiments are often repeated in La Tierra Amarilla. The speakers are small ranchers and farmers, most of whom work at other jobs but who nevertheless retain strong feelings for their land and their place on it. On weekdays they work for the Forest Service or the state highway department or teach or work at jobs in Española or Santa Fe. But many continue to work their ancestral lands in the evening after they have finished their jobs and on the weekends.

In recent years debates about water use and allocation in an arid land have commanded much attention throughout the Southwest. New Mexico, with its tricultural heritage based on Native American, Hispanic and Anglo-American traditions, is no exception. Conflicts arising over water use often threaten to separate this uneasy coalition. Issues such as the proper appropriation of ground waters, the relationship between poverty and access to water and the implications of subdivision developments for traditional water use have resulted in a flurry of studies, reports, recommendations and court cases. In La Tierra Amarilla a recent court case focused on the issue of the transfer of water rights and how such transfers might impair the rights of current users, and on the meaning of "public interest" as it pertains to water allocation.

Present in all these debates is the recognition of the historic role water has played in New Mexico Hispanic and Native American communities. Nowhere is this historic role more apparent than in the Hispanic villages of the high valleys of the upper Rio Grande and its tributaries. Water, and the land use it implies, is a central issue in La Tierra Amarilla in decisions about directions the future may take; it is the common denominator linking the past to the future.

It was the icy streams tumbling out of the Conejos Mountains and into the upper Chama Valley that first attracted herders to the area over 150 years ago. At the southern end of the valley where the first settlement occurred, two plateaus forming gentle steps from the steep hillsides to the valley floor below offered a natural drainage and permitted channeling of water across those table lands for agriculture and grazing. In the ensuing years the settlers developed a close relationship with La Tierra Amarilla. Land use patterns that emerged generations ago continue to shape the land despite a century of outside intrusions, including the loss of common graz-

54. Arid hillside, Parkview Community Ditch and fields, near Los Ojos.

ing lands, the shift from a barter to a cash economy, the Great Depression and the homogenizing pressures of twentieth century American culture. A close look at the historic bond between land and water and people suggests that despite these many outside challenges, this relationship persists. Moreover, this resilient bond between the people and their land and water may enable the descendants of those early settlers to sustain their culture even while adapting it to the realities of living in the global village.

The seventeenth and eighteenth century settlers on the northern frontier of New Mexico were primarily herders, who often traded livestock to the Pueblos for agricultural products. Never realizing their dreams of finding valuable ores, they subsisted on their remote and vulnerable estates, or *encomiendas*, sending meager yearly shipments of raw hides, buffalo robes, piñon nuts, blankets and Indian slaves down the Camino Real to the wealthy Mexican heartland. The limited varieties of vegetables that they raised consisted of radishes, lettuce, cucumbers, onions, garlic, peppers, beans and squash. Additionally, they raised various grains and grasses for pasturage, a practice that would become increasingly important in the late nineteenth century as common grazing lands began to be lost. To raise these crops the settlers used a gravity-based irrigation system, or *acequia*, a practice dating back to the water technology that the Moors introduced to Spain. The term derives from the Arabic stem "saqa," meaning "to water" or "to draw water," which later evolved to "al saqiya," denoting a water wheel or irrigation ditch.

As the Spanish settled the New World, they recognized the importance of the *acequias*, mentioning them in the Laws of the Indies of 1576 — the rules controlling new settlement. Legal title to land grants was generally based upon the grantees occupying and improving the land. Since most petitioners for grants stated their intent to cultivate the land, the availabilty of water for irrigation was an important consideration. Governors and *alcaldes*, or administrative justices, often assumed that water was present, but on some occasions they insisted that the lands be examined to determine their suitability for irrigation before the governor would issue the grant or the *alcalde* would sign the conveyance. Later, during the eighteenth century, the *alcalde* would often accompany the grantees to the grant and divide the irrigable land among the individual settlers. Such practices illustrate the importance colonial Spain placed on water and the role of irrigation in frontier settlement.[1]

The Plan of Pitic of 1713, which prescribed settlement plans for Spain's interior provinces, offered more specific provisions dealing with water rotation among users, community responsibility in maintaining ditches and local governance of the ditches. Although these prescriptions were rarely followed to the letter, they did provide the community *acequias* with the basis for community decision-making and a precedent open to local elaboration. Along the far-flung Spanish-Mexican frontier, the institution of the community *acequia* often served as the underlying foundation uniting families and sustaining settlements in the absence of local government and village priests. By 1848 and the annexation of New Mexico to the United States, the institution of the *acequia* was well established. The interim military jurisdiction, the

55. Ensenada Community Ditch, east of Ensenada.

Kearny Code of 1846, recognized the importance of this institution and stipulated that Mexican water laws would remain in effect.[2]

During the late nineteenth century, a series of New Mexico territorial legislative acts continued to recognize and codify *acequia* operations. The broad traditional powers of the ditch boss, or *mayordomo,* which had once encompassed control over the entire operation of the *acequia,* were divided between the *mayordomo* and the ditch association commissioners, or *comisionados,* the former being responsible for ditch maintenance and water dispersal and the latter receiving legal powers to enter into contracts and to assess penalties to delinquent members. Through all of these changes, however, the historical importance of the ditch and its role in the community remained intact. The prevailing attitude was that, in the words of turn-of-the-century lawyer and leading New Mexican historian R.E. Twitchell, the law always "stood guard for the perpetuation of the ancient systems of irrigation practiced in the country."[3]

Although La Tierra Amarilla was among the last-settled Hispanic frontiers, the first Spanish explorers to record their impression of the area – the Dominguez-Escalante expedition of 1776 – had noted the land's farming potential "with help of irrigation." When the original permanent settlers came north from Abiquiu in 1860-1861, seeking to settle the land granted to them in the Mexican grant of 1832, they immediately set to work developing irrigation systems. Water from the Chama River, and from the important tributaries, the Rio Brazos and Rito de Tierra Amarilla, then known as the Nutritas, was channeled to fields they had divided and laid out for crops. Despite the threat of attack from nearby Utes and Jicarillas, the settlers chose to fend for themselves, caring more about their cultivated fields than about matters of collective security. As a result, while defensible strongholds were built along the bluffs at Los Brazos and Los Ojos, many early homesteads and houses later built by the settlers' offspring were located near the fields.

The linear settlement pattern that emerged in the villages of La Tierra Amarilla underscores how important the *acequias* and the fields they irrigated were to shaping the early landscape. In the village of Tierra Amarilla, for example, although the *acequia* bisects the heart of the village, the vast majority of older houses extend along the edges of the irrigated fields, radiating west from the village along *La Cordillera* or northwest along the road to Los Ojos and Ensenada. Both roads are peripheral to the fields irrigated by the Tierra Amarilla Community Ditch. Houses and mobile homes that deviate from this pattern are of more recent construction, dating from after World War II. Their location, sometimes within the narrow fields themselves, serves as a reminder of how economic and social change have taken their toll on the earlier agricultural landscape.

56. Plaza Blanca Community Ditch, near Plaza Blanca.

A more pristine example of how irrigation helped to shape the land use appears in the village of Plaza Blanca. Founded in the mid-1870s, a generation after the other villages in the area, Plaza Blanca consists of a series of houses on a level contour overlooking the village's *acequia* and the irrigated fields below. Viewed from the hillside above the village, Plaza Blanca shows the fundamental Hispanic organization of space into a progression of long field strips stretching from the river up to the *acequia*; then the road fronting the village houses; next the villagers' houses with corrals framed by barns, sheds and fences behind; and finally the arid, uncultivated common lands.

The early community *acequias* at Tierra Amarilla, Los Ojos, La Puente and Ensenada, constructed between the years 1862-1865, became the arteries that sustained and nurtured the villages of La Tierra Amarilla. Even when the settlers and their descendants lost most of their common lands as a result of the quiet title case in 1883, the ditches which sometimes crossed the forfeited lands continued to be recognized as an essential part of the communities' agricultural and economic livelihood. In fact, the *acequias* defined many of the boundaries for the Catron exclusions during that quiet title suit. The ditches and the fields they irrigated stood as indisputable evidence of the improvements two generations of settlers had made on the land.

———

The *acequias* were built by men using wooden hand implements and oxen-drawn plows. Climbing up wooded canyons two to four miles above the plateaus they hoped to irrigate, the settlers diverted waters from mountain streams, seeking to create a gravity flow in which water would drop thirty to forty feet to the mile. Following the contours of the land, they would plow a furrow with a small stream of water trailing behind them to soften the hard, dry earth for digging. Herding responsibilities and the threat of Indian attacks added to the difficulty of early ditch digging as much as did the natural obstacles of trees, large rocks and arroyos. The results of these early efforts are a series of ditches that conform to the natural landscape and topography, flowing in sometimes ingenious patterns as they make their way to the field systems below. Here the ditch skirts an old tree or a flume carries water over a deep arroyo; there an old pickup door lines the *acequia* wall, directing the water into a culvert beneath a roadway. Thus, the *acequia* achieves a harmony with its surroundings, flowing, in the words of one long-time ditch user, "not too fast, not too slow" toward the cultivated acreage.

The remarkable technology underlying this system of Hispanic folk irrigation becomes apparent in the patterns of the fields as well — particularly in aerial photographs, but also to the roadside observer. Arranged in long rectangles, each with a slight slope to facilitate complete water coverage, the fields run lengthwise along the *acequia* or one of its laterals, known as *sangrias* or *contras acequias.* Originally measured in units called *varas* (about thirty-two inches), the fields were planned in such a way that all who possessed land might have access to water. When the colonial *alcalde* made the initial distribution of land among the settlers, he would assign each family a field ranging from fifty to 200 *varas* wide, depending on the

57. Ditch and lateral diversion, Ensenada.

58. Truck door and culvert, Plaza Blanca.

width of the irrigable valley at each point. In effect, it was this right to water and the land that it would irrigate that formed a primary community bond in the Spanish frontier settlement. All community members shared in a right to the life-giving water, and all bore the responsibility for maintaining the *acequia.* So important was this right that fields were divided lengthwise among heirs, creating fields of varying widths. Over generations many fields have also changed hands, creating a patchwork of ownership across the valley. It is not unusual to find fields just thirty or forty feet wide but extending several hundred yards in length from the *acequia.* At first, divisions were marked simply by weed breaks or field corner stone pyramids, known as *majotes,* and perhaps by a harvesting path. Today fences divide the fields, although properties are still punctuated by landmark trees and weed breaks as well.

The *acequia's* course is as apparent as the field boundary lines. Small berms of mud and silt, the result of the annual spring cleaning, line the ditch. During the summer these banks are covered with a lush growth of coneflower, thistle, goldenrod, penstemon, wild spinach, bullrush, sedge and purslane as well as whatever grains and grasses have migrated over the years from the fields into the *acequia.* Red willows and water hemlock also grow in clumps along the berms, particularly away from the fields themselves as when the Tierra Amarilla and Ensenada ditches pass through the centers of the villages. For many ditches in New Mexico the presence of willows, cottonwoods and other heavy water-using species has led the ditch associations to line the ditches with concrete to avoid water loss. In the case of the ditches of La Tierra Amarilla, however, no such attempt has been made because of the ample yearly runoff and because many members view the costs as prohibitive. Four of the five community ditches do have concrete headgates, however, for diverting water into the ditch.

Other patterns also emerge in this landscape mosaic. Along the fences and ditches are worn paths used by farmers to get to their sometimes far-flung fields. A single plank or two aspen logs lashed together may denote a bridge, and a length of leather harness and piece of wood clasping two juniper fence posts may signal a gate. At the lowest corner of the field system, rivulets of surplus water descending through lush greenery to the valley floor mark the ditch's runoff channel, known as the *desagüe.* Often this surplus will simply drain back into the river, as it does in the case of the Tierra Amarilla ditch, which drains back into Rito de Tierra Amarilla, or the Plaza Blanca ditch, which drains into the Rio Chama. But in other instances, the excess waters from an *acequia* at a higher elevation may simply drop into a lower *acequia,* as is the case of the Parkview ditch surplus water which flows into the La Puente ditch.

59. Abandoned concrete headgate, east of Tierra Amarilla.

60. New headgate foreground, old gate background, east of Tierra Amarilla.

With the nearby Conejos Mountains to the east providing a usually bountiful snowshed, surplus runoffs are not uncommon. One unfortunate consequence of having this ample supply of moisture has been a chronic problem with spring flooding. During such floods the Rio Chama and Rio Brazos often change their course across their stony floodplains, and sometimes the rivers shift away from the ditch headgates. For ditches with concrete headgates, such shifts mean that ditch members, or *parciantes*, must hire heavy equipment or work themselves to rechannel the river back into the headgate. In the case of the Plaza Blanca ditch, which still uses a wooden headgate to draw waters from the Rio Chama, members have had to repair or even relocate their headgate frequently during recent years because of the unusually high runoffs. To do this the *mayordomo* and his helpers must don high rubber boots and redirect a channel from the river, placing boughs, tree trunks and rocks along its side in the hope that the next high waters will not undo their work.

Changing river courses have also affected field patterns, particularly those of low-lying fields along the valley floor. The village of Plaza Blanca, the only community of the west bank of the Chama, was created by what Kutsche and VanNess call the "budding process."[4] Settled in the 1880s by the descendants of the area's original settlers, the village's fields seem to be a lower extension of the fields surrounding the village of La Puente, which is perched forty feet above the river's east bank. Early maps show fields paralleling each other with the same family names on either side of the river. As the Chama has eroded away its east bank, it has reduced the length of some of the La Puente fields and extended the lengths of those in Plaza Blanca well into the west bank's grove of cottonwoods, known as the *bosque.*

Just as the *acequias* help to define the land use patterns in La Tierra Amarilla, they also shape the patterns of seasonal work.[5] Traditionally April is the month for cleaning the ditches. On an appointed date the *parciantes* gather to work their way down the ditch. They are directed by the *mayordomo*, who measures out a section of ditch of approximately ten feet, known as a *tarea*, for each worker to clean. In recent years backhoe operators have been hired for ditch cleaning work. As a result, many ditch associations no longer expect their full membership to participate in the spring cleaning. In La Tierra Amarilla, for instance, only the Plaza Blanca Ditch Association still cleans its ditch without a backhoe. Many long-time ditch users feel that this labor-saving measure has brought with it the hidden cost of weakening members' link with the community, diminishing the sense of responsibility that each member once felt as he worked alongside his fellow ditch member shoveling the ditch clean.

Later, during May, June and early July, when the ditch is full and the crops are growing, a common sight is a pickup parked along a road and a solitary, shovel-carrying figure with high rubber boots trudging along a distant field edge to turn water from the *acequia* into his land. During seasons with plentiful runoff, there is little problem with all *parciantes* having enough water, and they can irrigate freely. But in dry seasons it becomes the responsibility of the *mayordomo* to allocate water and the times when users may turn it into their fields. He must walk the ditch, making sure that there are no leaks and that the water is flowing unimpeded. Sometimes, during a high runoff, he may need to journey several miles above the fields to clean the river channel leading into the headgate. By late summer the water flow decreases as the snow melt ends, and afternoon rains provide what moisture is needed. Soon the fields are cut and the grasses are baled for use as winter fodder. Then sheep and cattle are moved from their summer pastures in the mountains to forage in the fenced fields. By late summer the *acequia* has served its purpose, and the *mayordomo* will lower the headgate, turning most of the water back into the stream. Some water is left to flow in the ditch, however, because many local wells are charged by ditch waters.

During the fall and winter, decaying vegetation and a season's accumulation of silt clog the ditches. While much of this detritus will be removed with the spring cleaning, some of it will remain and flow with the water into the fields, providing a natural source of fertilizer and nutrients. At some specified date during the winter months, the *parciantes* will meet to elect new *comisionados* and a new *mayordomo* for the next season. And the cycle goes on. In recent years, as economic change has driven some residents to other jobs and as technological change has led to the availability of backhoes, active membership in the ditch associations has declined. Nevertheless, those who do remain active, and even those whose circumstances have taken them out of the valley for work, continue to look upon the *acequia* and the responsibility it implies as an essential part of their cultural heritage.

One important consequence of the development of the local *acequias* was the agricultural successes La Tierra Amarilla experienced during the three decades prior to World War I, a factor contributing to the commercial and residential growth of the two major villages, Los Ojos and Tierra Amarilla. Although logging and the outfitting of fortune hunters heading north into the San Juan gold fields had contributed to the area's earlier economic growth, agriculture and livestock provided the basis of the economy. In the 1910 United States Department of Agriculture census report, thirty-six percent of all farm acreage in the New Mexico Territory was listed as gravity irrigated.[6] Yet so important was this practice locally that Rio Arriba County was reported as having ninety-six percent of all its agriculture gravity irrigated, the highest proportion in the territory. The county ranked first in the territory in cut green grain, second in dry bean and pea production, and third in wheat and barley;

———

61. Aerial view of the field systems of Tierra Amarilla, 1981. Photo by Paul Logsdon.

2-B

B Julio Ulibarri 22.4 ac.

A George Becker 64.0 ac.

To Parkview

Puente Community Ditch

Boundary of "G" Tract-Catron Exclusions–
Tierra Amarilla Grant–"6-G" Cor.

"7-G" Cor.

57 Jose Abayta 16.0 ac

56 J.M. Truillo 9.0 ac.

55

54 Gom. Salazar 12.1 ac

53 J.M. Truillo 9.0 ac.

52 J.J. Manzanares 14.1 ac

51 Tircio Gomez 19.0 ac

50 J.M. Truillo 9.0 ac.

49 Antonio Lopez 18.9 ac

48 Saralle Serrano 9.3 ac.

47

46 S.M. Lopez - 5.3 ac.

45 Pablo Alire - 6.0 ac.

44 Pablo Alire - 5.5 ac.

43 J.J. Manzanares - 5.0 ac.

42 J.J. Manzanares 6.1 ac

42A

41A Plaza of Puente 14 ac

40A

41 Lopez

40

39

38

37 Tobias Attencio - 13.0 ac.

36 S.M. Truillo - 6 ac

35 Gom. Salazar

62

61

60

Road

CHAMA RIVER

To Tierra Amarilla

"8-G" Cor.

"9-G" Cor.

To Plaza Blanca

Lot 9 Tircio Gomez

NORTH

2-B Mrs. Ant. Lopez 3.0 ac.
55 Ed Cordova sold to J.J. Manzanares 3.8 ac.
62 1.3 acres
61 S.M. Lopez 0.7 ac.
60 S.M. Truillo 1.1 ac.
47 2.5 ac. Placedos Salazar
42A Sandoval sold to Oct. Manzanares - 1.2 acres
40A Leandro Montanyo 3.0 ac
40 1.9 ac Lopez
38 Gom. Salazar sold to Mrs. J.M. Truillo 4.4 ac.

62. Map of the La Puente irrigation and field
system by Kenneth A. Heron, 1924. Redrawn
from original in the State Engineer's Office.
Irrigated area shaded.

it was also high in sheep and wool production. Oral tradition recalls annual trading of livestock and potatoes and grain, which grew well in the high elevations of La Tierra Amarilla, for fruits and vegetables from the lower-lying Española and Abiquiu areas, closer to Santa Fe.

Yet even as this diverse agriculture was thriving in La Tierra Amarilla, factors undermining it were at work. The widespread fencing of the grant's common lands, which began to the north toward Chama after 1912, meant that livestock could no longer roam the once common grazing lands. Many local stock owners engaged in a form of livestock sharecropping, the *partido* system, in which they borrowed sheep from wool brokers and merchants to increase their herds and then repaid them, usually with wool and twenty-five percent of the lambs produced. As the availability of common grazing land decreased, local grazers found themselves able to increase their herds only at the cost of overgrazing the rangeland and limiting crops in their fields to those offering winter fodder. The problems posed by an already declining wool market were exacerbated in the 1920s when access to the Carson National Forest was limited as the Forest Service began to pursue land management policies designed to restore the overgrazed and eroding forest lands. By the 1930s, when the Bureau of Indian Affairs also adopted more restrictive grazing policies on Indian lands, the days of the great local sheep herds ended. Gone were the days that old-timers, or *viejitos*, recall in which herds numbering in the thousands came down from the high summer pastures to be turned into the fields that served as a fall common pasturage. Gone were the days of renting the warmer, lower elevation lands of the Navajos for winter pasture. Gone with the sheep was much of the residents' self-sufficiency based on the wool for weaving, the food and the fertilizer those animals provided. In their place appeared small herds of cattle that local ranchers grazed on forest lands using permits and then sold.

63. Arid hillside and irrigated field near La Puente.

64. Abandoned farm equipment, near Plaza Blanca.

The agricultural depression that followed World War I also affected local agriculture and, ultimately, the landscape. No longer able simply to subsist in what had become a cash economy, local men were forced to leave the valley in increasing numbers to find wage work in the mines and mills of Colorado, on the railroad, in the forests, and as cowhands on the big ranches of Wyoming. In their absence untended livestock threatened the irrigated fields. In response the fields were fenced, signaling a break with the communal feeling that had marked earlier agricultural practices. With the fences the traditional practice of permitting all of the community members' stock to graze on the stubble of the harvested private fields also disappeared.[7] Soon the informal crop rotation practices in which a part of one field was given over to vegetables were abandoned. Likewise, with the mechanization of agriculture in the 1930s and the collapse of the sheep market, the practice of using sheep to fertilize the fields in the fall and to stimulate the growth of spring grain crops by aerating the soil with their sharp pointed hooves fell into disuse. Yet the promise of large-scale mechanized farming went unfulfilled, for the small, narrow, remote fields and the fragile earthen *sangrias* irrigating them made the use of large combines and harvesters impractical.

As a result of these factors, agriculture and the local economy have languished since the Depression. The prevailing attitude among outsiders has been to look at the villages of La Tierra Amarilla as vestiges of an outdated agricultural system — as an unintended living museum. Scenic — yes; interesting — yes; practical — no. In this age of escalating recreationalism, once the eye scans the patchwork of fields along the valley floor and the clusters of buildings in the villages, the temptation is to shift one's focus to the Brazos Peaks, where on a nearby hillside a ski run has already been cut and, hidden on the wooded slopes, subdivisions of summer homes are beginning to appear.

Yet, to embrace these developments at the cost of overlooking the houses, fields, and *acequias* suggests a myopia that threatens the rich texture of the region's rural landscape. In tracing the history of *acequias* in the Southwest, Michael C. Myer uses the term "ecolturation" to denote the means by which settlers adapted to the ecological system they encountered upon settling a new area, shaping the landscape and an agricultural economy as a response to the new land.[8] That evolutionary process occurred during the first three generations of occupation in La Tierra Amarilla, enabling the early residents to combine raising of livestock, which they grazed on common lands, with agriculture, based on their system of small but carefully

65. Ensenada Community Ditch.

66. El Barranco Community Ditch, near Los Brazos.

67. Desagüe of El Porvenir Ditch, near Ensenada.

managed fields. It also provided a means by which villagers could work together as what one writer calls a "quasi cooperative."[9] The loss of common lands and the shift to a wage economy weakened that system, removing an important community resource and substituting a value system that worked against community cooperation.

Despite these setbacks, many area residents continue to work their fields and to own livestock, often in combination with some outside income-earning job. A local schoolteacher raises alfalfa and a small flock of sheep, much as his grandfather did; a retired county official continues his family's tradition of cattle-raising and feeds them with his own timothy and alfalfa; numerous villagers who work in the resorts in the nearby village of Chama return each evening to turn water from the *sangrias* into their fields. If they do not raise stock themselves, at least they can sell the cut green grasses across the border in Colorado to earn a few extra dollars, which is important in this region of chronic underemployment. Such efforts suggest that the local process of "ecolturation" is continuing. They also suggest that many of the people of La Tierra Amarilla recognize the reality of surviving in a cash economy but at the same time are searching for a way by which they may retain what is valuable from their past — their relationship to the resources of land and water.

4 — Learning from the Past

La Tierra Amarilla is a land rich in its architectural and land use traditions. To travel through this upland valley is to travel well beyond mainstream American culture into a culture that has managed to retain its identity to a remarkable degree, despite the momentum toward modernization that tends to obliterate the past. It is the upland valleys, such as La Tierra Amarilla, that contribute so much to the regional identity of the American Southwest, conveying the sense that this region, this place, is somehow different and worth experiencing — and celebrating — for its difference.

But maintaining a distinctive local culture amidst the homogenizing pressures of mass culture is a constant struggle. The history of La Tierra Amarilla reflects how easily a dominant culture can threaten a fragile one. Within two generations after settlement, the trinity of land, water and people was disrupted. A sense of community, rooted in cooperation and in access to common lands, was disrupted. Moreover, the settlers' very outlook was challenged. Underlying the individual's participation in community life had been an attitude that one writer describes as a "self-effacing probity that restrained him [the Hispanic Villager] from advancing himself at the expense of others."[1] Known as *vergüenza*, this outlook subordinated individual aggrandizement, deferring to the good of a community that was based upon shared resources. With the coming of early developers, land and water were no longer looked upon as communal resources but were seen instead as commodities to be bought and sold on the open market. Because of this radically different view of land use, not only did the people lose their common lands as the community land grant fell into private hands, but the very foundation of their value system was undermined.

The advent of a wage economy further disrupted the sense of community. People gave up their subsistence agricultural practices and sought work that rewarded them with money that they could use to purchase necessities, many of which they had previously produced for themselves. Men left the valley to find work, and often when they were unable to earn enough they sold the one thing they possessed that was of value — their remaining parcels of land. In making these shifts in their lives, people began to modify many proven practices from their past, including crop rotation. As they moved away in pursuit of jobs, they abandoned many old houses and barns. Fields were let go or were simply used to graze a few cows or horses.

A few traditional houses were built after World War Two, but the static population created no great demand for new construction. In recent years, many young

---

68. Casados House, Los Ojos, built about 1885.

people have preferred to purchase a mobile home, which comes with easy financing and a full set of modern conveniences. Many mobile homes stand beside ancestral houses gradually disintegrating in the elements. Federal funding for housing, while it was still available, was directed into a HUD tract development of standard houses rather than being used to recondition existing houses. Some disaster relief funds that became available after a severe winter and a hail storm both about 1980, did go to covering many older houses with red anodized roofing.

But the local building tradition does continue in a handful of owner-built homes. One house, for instance, is under construction by Gumercindo Salazar of La Puente, a junior high computer and math teacher, a sheep rancher and founding member of the Los Ganados cooperative. He began to build anew after the house erected by his

69. HUD housing, north of Tierra Amarilla, built in 1970s.

70. Gumercindo Salazar House, La Puente, under construction late 1980s.

grandfather (and discussed in chapter two) was destroyed by fire early in this decade. The new house is of wood frame construction, with a layer of insulation inside and, outside, a layer of adobes, many of which were salvaged from his grandfather's house. The ground floor is a basic two-bedroom ranch style plan with oversized kitchen and living room, ample enough to accommodate a large family fiesta. The upper level, though, has the traditional half-story design, with wall dormers and a gable-end door.

The US 84 bypass, which cuts through the valley on its raised bed, like the mobile homes symbolizes the outside values and forces that have pressured the local culture. Dropping into the bowl-like valley from Santa Fe to the south, the highway shoots on a straight course north toward Chama. Green and white signs mark the turnoffs for the more important villages; the smaller ones are overlooked. Unobtrusively, the older highway snakes from village to village, criss-crossing the bypass, and follows the natural contours of the land. Midway through the valley, the new highway drops from the upper to the lower plateau and bisects the fields irrigated by the Parkview Ditch. While the fields' fences meet the highway at oblique angles, they align with each other on either side of the road, the alignment a reminder of the once contiguous single units. In one field sits a mobile home, in another a ranch-style home. The highway and the structures alongside stand in marked contrast to the villages and fields in the distance. Together, the two constitute a pattern of old and new, a palimpsest in which the lines of the recent highway system are drawn over the field lines and roads of the earlier land use system.

The temptation is to look only at the latest marks on the landscape and to read them as the harbingers of progress. Such evidence underscores in some minds the belief that the decline in farming has created a social and economic disintegration that makes La Tierra Amarilla ripe for a big project — that its wooded slopes are ready for a ski resort and its waters are ready for diversion to dude ranch trout ponds. In fact, many developers see their projects as the key to an economic

71. Highway bypass and broken fields, east of Los Ojos.

redevelopment of the area. They point to the construction and service jobs that such projects will create. Thus many are surprised when their plans meet with local opposition from ditch associations and other community organizations. They find it difficult to believe that these villagers are, in the words of one activist, unwilling "to scuttle their past and turn over their ancestral lands and water in order to progress."

It is the community concern over preserving these residual elements that has galvanized a growing opposition to imported projects. In the 1985 Encinias case concerning the diversion of ditch waters from agricultural to recreational uses, expert witnesses emphasized the cultural value of these older water use institutions. Echoes of Peter van Dresser's warnings of twenty years ago, in which he envisioned a threat of "painfully artificial playgrounds" that would reduce the cultural landscape to "sterile and institutional bleakness," resound in the testimony of the opposition.[2]

A number of other recent decisions have aided the cause of cultural preservation. In 1976, the National Forest Management Act mandated that the administrators of local National Forests develop a management plan that they update every ten years with public input and review. In response to this decision National Forests located in New Mexico have moved toward policy statements such as that of the Santa Fe National Forest, which recognizes "the economic and social needs of the people of Northern New Mexico" and seeks "to maintain and enrich cultural values and a viable rural economy."

In 1985, citizens of the area were asked to respond to a county proposal for tough new subdivision ordinances that will force developers to obtain water rights subject to review by the State Engineer's Office before going ahead on projects. In 1987, the state legislature passed a bill that earmarks funds for the renovation of the state's historic *acequias*. The voicing of such sentiments indicates that government agencies far-removed from La Tierra Amarilla and the other mountain valleys are beginning to recognize the needs of these distant constituents as well. Such responses also indicate a growing recognition that an uncritical embrace of progress can diminish the richness of a culture by attenuating its differences, that the fabric that is American society would be duller, less poignant, if this landscape and these folkways were to vanish.

The people of La Tierra Amarilla are encouraged by the formulation of a public policy that is sympathetic with their struggle to sustain their cultural roots. They are encouraged to see that the long-standing tradition of state and federal support of new businesses and large-scale ranching may now be extended to them as well. They also hope, however, that these policy planners will recognize the cultural and historical resources that already exist, that they will detect the older lines of the palimpsest. They hope that future planning will be able to augment and nurture the local efforts that the people have begun in order to help themselves.

The first impetus for locally controlled economic development came from La Clinica, the nonprofit, community-based clinic staffed by doctors of the National Health Service. Founded in 1970, La Clinica addressed a chronic problem facing much of rural America, the absence of local, trained health care. In the early years, the clinic's doctors found that many health problems were stress related. Moreover, they found that this stress was induced by anxieties over unemployment and the loss of economic self-sufficiency. In effect, the loss of land and a way of life was mirrored internally in medical problems.

Thus, the first challenge facing visionary community members was to find ways to bolster the local economy that would restore pride and self-confidence. The initial response was to try innovative programs. One project involved construction of a number of greenhouse additions for the production of vegetables and heat. Another project sought to encourage cattle and hog raising. But these efforts were unsuc-

72. House with 1970s greenhouse addition, La Puente.

73. Churro Sheep, Los Ganados flock. Photo by Carolyn Kinsman.

cessful because, it was felt, they were conceived on too grand a scale and did not build sufficiently upon local experience. Community activists learned an important lesson from these attempts, however. First, they realized that state agricultural extension services are geared toward large-scale commercial farmers and ranchers and are of little help in meeting the agricultural needs of small upland valleys. Second, they learned from the writings of planners such as Hazel Henderson and E.F. Schumacher that small-scale economic development offered an approach more viable to the realities of La Tierra Amarilla.[3] Given the pattern of small fields as well as the pattern of employment embracing seasonal and part-time work, a project must also fit into the local scale to succeed. In effect, the vision for a better future was informed by the past.

This latest step in the evolving process of "ecolturation" appears in the form of Los Ganados del Valle, a cooperative of approximately forty shareholders founded and run by local farmers, ranchers, spinners and weavers. Several members work at other jobs, but all identify strongly with the land and are seeking to revitalize traditional land uses and crafts by employing modern agricultural and business practices. According to its charter, Los Ganados' goal is to "create new business opportunities as well as conserve a unique way of life." To realize this goal the cooperative has developed other businesses and programs, including a weavers' cooperative, known as Tierra Wools, and a summer art program for children. In the years since 1983, when Los Ganados was founded, it has emerged as a model of how people can adapt and work together to hold on to what they value from their past. Noting how members of the cooperative are able to work together, one rancher observes, "We've all belonged to ditch associations and know that cooperation works for all."

———

Building their flocks to 1,500 sheep, Los Ganados ranchers have reintroduced the hardy Churro breed, whose long staple, low grease wool is ideal for the needs of the weavers at Tierra Wools. The ranchers have also adapted yearly grazing cycles to the traditional land use patterns of the valley. For the summer months, they hire a herder to tend the flock and move it across rented grazing lands. While the sheep are in high country pastures, Los Ganados ranchers work in their own fields and others that they lease, turning waters into them for irrigation and then cutting the hay, which they use to feed their flock in winter. In the fall they bring the sheep back into the valley, turning them onto the fields to forage on the remaining grasses. Members note that this practice has benefitted the fields, for the urine and manure of the sheep has increased the vitality of the following summer's crops. Despite the success of these grazing practices, problems remain for although the villages are surrounded by lands granted to the ancestors of many of the Ganados ranchers, they have encountered difficulty securing adequate, dependable summer grazing.

Some of the legal background to the loss of these common lands is recounted in the first chapter on Tierra Amarilla history. That story is part of the general failure of the United States government to fulfill one provision of the 1848 Treaty of Guadalupe Hidalgo with Mexico. In that treaty, Mexico ceded most of the Southwest to the United States, while the U.S. promised, among other things, to respect the property rights of Mexican citizens in this territory. To a great degree, the Tijerina incident of 1967 and, more recently, the Amador Flores case in which

74. Suzanna Ulibarri, apprentice weaver, spinning at Tierra Wools, 1988. Photo by Maureen Schein, *Rio Grande Sun*.

Mr. Flores has refused to surrender common lands he claims belong to the heirs of the Tierra Amarilla Land Grant, reflect the frustrations of some local people with the government's failure to redress these injustices.

Pueblo Indians and Hispanic land grant heirs have fared differently under the U.S. government. The creation of reservations based on land grants made earlier by the Spanish government did much to protect the land base of Indian Pueblos. Some Pueblo lands did fall into non-Pueblo hands in the late nineteenth and early twentieth century, however, through questionable practices. But Congress established the Indian Claims Commission to address this situation, and between 1932 and 1978, it returned two-thirds of a million acres to the Pueblos and compensated the non-Pueblo owners for this land.[4]

Historian Donald Cutter has suggested that a Hispanic Land Claims Commission, patterned on the Indian Claims Commission, be established to address disputes in the handling of the land grants. Such a commission might be empowered to purchase and return lands or to make cash payments to grant heirs. Malcolm Ebright, who studied the history of the Tierra Amarilla grant, has added that since the courts refuse to hear most land grant claims because of previous congressional and judicial actions, only such a commission, established by Congress, could reopen this question. This possibility was also raised in the fall of 1988, at hearings of the House Interior and Insular Affairs Committee concerning Mexican and Spanish Land Grants in Northern New Mexico which were conducted by Representatives Samuel Gejdenson (D-CT) and Bill Richardson (D-NM).[5]

William deBuys, a historian of land use in northern New Mexico, has noted that widespread restitution of land grants is a political impossibility because it would "cast doubt on the legitimacy of ownership of vast tracts of land from the Gulf of Mexico to the Pacific Ocean." DeBuys also adds that, "to apportion ownership equitably between present residents and the many legitimate heirs who long since moved would tax the wisdom of a thousand Solomons."[6]

Since former common lands are in question, any recompense might go not to individual descendants but the local community. Such funds or lands could be managed by a cooperative or corporation controlled by descendants who still live on the land grant at least part time. The primary objective of such corporations might be, not the production of small annual dividends for all heirs, but instead the stimulation of local economic development. This approach would more nearly honor the Spanish tradition of access to the resources of the commons based on participation in the community. It would also begin to address the chronic poverty of so many of the land grant villages through local control of a resource base rather than through government support.

———

75. Men working on San Jose Church, Los Ojos, August 1935. Photo by Fr. Gerard Geier.

Another approach to this problem, suggested by William deBuys, would use the Forest Service planning process to ensure that common lands under that agency's control are managed for the social and economic benefit of the land grant villages. This could be a positive step, and as deBuys suggests, it may be more politically and economically feasible than a lands commission. But this approach still leaves the land grant descendants obligated to the federal government and deprives them of the self-determination that is an essential underpinning of cultural vitality. Besides, this approach is not a possibility for the Tierra Amarilla grant and the many other grants that are largely in private hands rather than under Forest Service control.[7]

The only currently unallocated grazing lands near the valley's villages are located in two wildlife preserves administered by the State Fish and Game Department. These lands were deeded to the state by the Nature Conservancy with the stipulation that they be used solely as a wildlife habitat. Los Ganados ranchers have suggested a small, trial grazing program on these lands so they can demonstrate to skeptical public land management officials that careful herding practices in which a herder frequently moves his sheep can actually stimulate vegetative growth rather than destroy it. But as some environmentalists have noted, the Savory system, which Los Ganados proposes to employ, can be a success but only with expert day-to-day management. Los Ganados, nevertheless, feels that, given an opportunity to prove their management abilities through this pilot grazing project, they can resolve their ongoing problem of securing steady grazing lands. This approach has the same limitations as deBuys's similar Forest Service planning proposal, but like that proposal is a promising first step.

—

76. Tierra Wools showroom, Los Ojos, 1983.

Yet a final possibility would be for a foundation or the state or federal government to purchase grazing rights for Los Ganados to use in their trial grazing program. This would allow Los Ganados to prove their theories and management abilities, which, in turn, could provide a valuable model for economic development on the other land grants of northern New Mexico.

So successful has the Churro project already been that in response to distant buyers' inquiries, the cooperative has begun to stage the Rocky Mountain Specialty Sheep Show in Chama each spring. Moreover, in 1987 Los Ganados paid off its start-up loans. In realizing these economic successes, Los Ganados has preserved not only aspects the area's traditional land use practices but a landmark building as well. Although many of the weavers work at looms in their homes, Tierra Wools' office and store at located in the T.D. Burns Mercantile building in Los Ojos. Closed for over a decade and falling into disrepair as adobe buildings will do in this land of harsh winters, the structure was bought by the cooperative in 1984, established through local efforts, and is now listed on the National Register of Historic Places. In 1988, the cooperative embarked on an ambitious project of installing machinery to wash and scour wool so that, except for carding the wool, the entire process of transforming fresh-cut wool to woven goods might be accomplished on the premises. In restoring and then attaining recognition for this building, the members of Tierra Wools have demonstrated to other area residents how their buildings might become a part of their usable past.

As the weaving program has moved from infancy toward maturity and its products are sold in galleries throughout the Southwest, Tierra Wools has emerged as the fourth largest private employer in northern Rio Arriba County. An apprentice program has been initiated to provide even more local citizens with an economic opportunity. During the summer the cooperative began an Art for Kids course, enrolling fifteen local children in a program that led to the execution of several murals in Los Ojos. The visitor who takes time to stop in Los Ojos and to see the showroom of Tierra Wools Weavers can see much more than the finely woven blankets and garments of local crafts-people; the visitor can also see people busy at looms, as many of their ancestors once were, and engaged in a panoply of other jobs associated with running a small business. The sum of this activity is a community of workers making a small but positive step toward economic independence and dignity.

Other examples of pride in local heritage abound. In the village of Los Brazos a family has consolidated ownership of its two-story, fourteen-room ancestral house and opened a bed and breakfast. Older citizens who left the valley to find work in the 1930s and 1940s are returning upon their retirement to take up limited farming and, in some instances, to restore childhood homes. Ditch association members are taking a renewed interest in the ditches, realizing in the aftermath of the Encinas case that they will need to fight to protect their water. Some people are looking at their land and water and beginning to sense that it may no longer be necessary to reject

77. T.D. Burns Building, Home of Tierra Wools, Los Ojos, 1983.

their heritage in order to survive, that small-scale weekend ranching may be part of a viable alternative for surviving with their heritage intact. Reflecting on the possibilities that such a lifestyle affords, one Los Ganados member remarks, "Thirty years from now we hope to still be doing the same thing. I intend to."

Local social activism and self-help have long been a part of the community *acequia* systems of La Tierra Amarilla. This communal means of irrigation provided village members not only with a livelihood but with a sense of community responsibility and control. Today the efforts of Los Ganados del Valle and others offer growing evidence that local self-help institutions emphasizing small-scale but customized agriculture based on traditional water and land use practices can continue to ensure cultural continuity in La Tierra Amarilla.

78. High line lateral of the Tierra Amarilla Ditch and Santo Niño Church, Tierra Amarilla.

PART TWO: Introduction

*P*art Two of the book provides historical background and a discussion of the significance of each of the five registered historic villages, along with suggested driving tours, and descriptions of all registered properties both in the historic districts and outside.

The driving tours are designed for visitors and area residents alike as introductions to the architecture, settlement patterns, and irrigation systems of the valley. Only highly visible, representative buildings and landscape features are noted, while other, equally important examples abound in the area. Our hope is that once you have taken one or two of the tours, you will be more adept at reading historic buildings and the cultural landscape. Remember that only the county courthouse and a few commercial buildings are open to the public; all other buildings should be viewed only from the public road. Please respect people's privacy.

The listings of historic properties assign names to buildings, often the name of the builder, the first residents, or a family that occupied the building over a long period. If more than one name is known, the oldest name is given first. (Any corrections or additional information can be sent to the Historic Preservation Division.)

Property owners may be especially interested in the listings of registered properties. These include all of the buildings and irrigation systems in chapter ten, and all structures shown as contributing on the district maps. The written listings of district buildings also include a few non-contributing buildings, which were built before 1945, but have been modified to the extent that they have lost their historic integrity. Some contributing buildings are also listed as significant which means that they are of somewhat more historical or architectural importance than those only listed as contributing.

Owners of significant or contributing properties can receive publications and technical advice on building maintenance and preservation questions from the State Historic Preservation Division. Owners may also be eligible for State or Federal income tax credits for work they do on their buildings. The State credit for approved preservation work can be taken for half of expenses up to $25,000, and can be spread over as many as five years of tax liability. The Federal credit is restricted to income-producing properties and is generally used only for large projects. The state also recently established a revolving loan fund for preservation work. For further information or assistance contact the Historic Preservation Division, Office of Cultural Affairs, Villa Rivera, Room 101, 228 East Palace Avenue, Santa Fe, New Mexico 87503, phone (505) 827-8320.

——

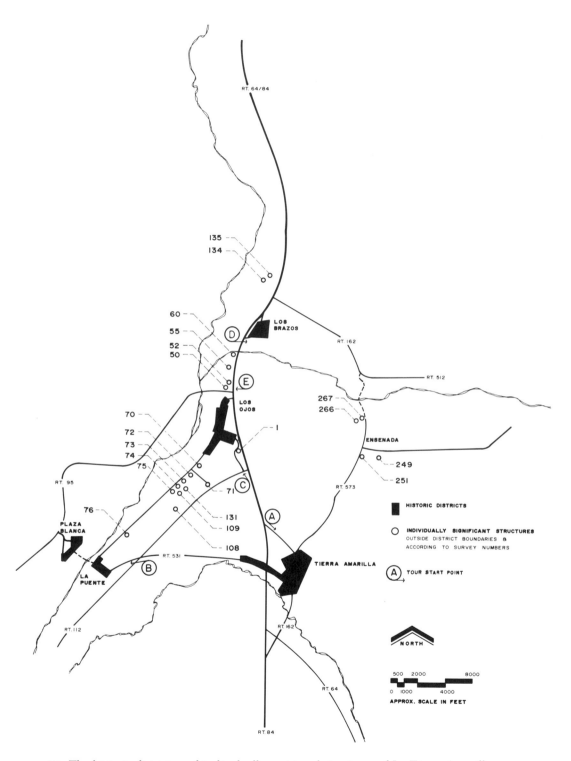

RT. 64/84

135
134

60
55
52
50

70
72
73
74
75

RT. 95

76

PLAZA
BLANCA

LA
PUENTE

RT. 112

LOS
BRAZOS

RT. 162

RT. 512

267
266

ENSENADA

249
251

RT. 573

71

131
109

108

RT. 531

LOS
OJOS

1

D

E

C

A

B

TIERRA AMARILLA

RT. 162

RT. 64

RT. 84

HISTORIC DISTRICTS

INDIVIDUALLY SIGNIFICANT STRUCTURES
OUTSIDE DISTRICT BOUNDARIES &
ACCORDING TO SURVEY NUMBERS

A   TOUR START POINT

NORTH

500   2000   8000
0   1000   4000
APPROX. SCALE IN FEET

79. The historic districts and individually registered structures of La Tierra Amarilla.

5 — *Tierra Amarilla*

rom its founding in 1860-61, Tierra Amarilla has been one of the two major settlements in the area, the other being Los Ojos, which was the early commercial and religious center. While Tierra Amarilla began as a farming village, the decision of T.D. Burns to build his home there in 1876 and later a store, and the territorial legislature's decision to locate the county seat there in 1880 led to the emergence of the village as the commercial and governmental center of the area. Although the Burns house and store have been demolished, several two-story residential and commercial structures and the courthouse built in 1917 serve as reminders of the village's prominence. Tierra Amarilla's houses include some fine examples of the basic New Mexican Hispanic folk tradition and of the local folk architecture which incorporated Anglo-American elements such as gable roofs with balconies, milled ornamentation, and the locally distinctive half-story wall. Six hipped-roof houses, four two-story structures, three buildings with center hall plans and facade symmetry, and the area's sole Free Classic Style building illustrate the far greater degree with which Tierra Amarilla builders embraced Anglo-American styles than did builders in the other villages. Additionally, several roadside commercial structures built in the Southwest Vernacular Style signify the importance of the village during the pre-World War II highway era. With its varied architecture and courthouse, its central commercial area and its radiating residential spokes, Tierra Amarilla mirrors the area's early settlement and adaptations to outside forces on the local landscape and culture.

Tierra Amarilla was first known as Las Nutritas, for the beavers which were once prevalent along the small creek of the same name. It was one of the first permanent settlements of the area. Its *acequia*, dating back to 1862, is the oldest one in the area that is recorded in the State Engineer's Office. Situated at the southeast entrance to the valley and with a broad plateau extending away to the west, nearby timbered slopes to the east, and a creek providing a steady stream of water to the south, the site was ideal for settlement. Although it is unclear to what degree the area designated in the 1921 State Engineer's map of the Tierra Amarilla as the "Plaza of Tierra Amarilla" was actually the early nucleus of the village, linear settlement patterns quickly emerged along roadways extending to the other villages. *La Cordillera*, or the La Puente road, provides a fine example of a line of homesteads placed along the lower edge of the fields system. Dating back to the 1860s and lined by houses uniformly employing the local folk architecture of linear self-contained rooms, gabled roofs, many with balconies, this spoke illustrates the readiness of mid-

—

80. T.D. Burns Store, Tierra Amarilla, built about 1910. Photo courtesy of Fr. Austin Ernst.

nineteenth-century Hispanic settlers to live near their fields and to derive a building style based both on tradition and newly available materials such as corrugated sheet metal and lumberyard wood ornamentation.

Although Los Ojos emerged as the first commercial center of the area, Tierra Amarilla began to surpass it by the 1880's. From 1872 to 1880 the Ute Indian Agency was located there. T.D. Burns, who had come to the area as a sutler in 1867, supplying beef to the agency and who, by 1900, would establish a network of stores ranging up to southern Colorado, built an elaborate home in Tierra Amarilla in 1876 and later added a store to the front of it. This development combined with the arrival of the railroad in Chama in 1880 and the availability of shipped goods and milled lumber, began a building boom in the village in which a number of prosperous Hispanic merchants built homes incorporating Anglo-American elements into the local tradition. The Jose R. Martinez house with its cupola, central hall plan, and cut wood ornaments, and the Archuleta store, a widened two-story gabled structure with an Anglo-American commercial facade and second-story central hall exemplify the trend.

Placing the county seat in Tierra Amarilla also brought a wide variety of government jobs to the village. Combined with the agricultural and commercial elements, so strong were these influences that by 1890 Max Frost would note that the entire area was "depending on Tierra Amarilla" for its direction. So important was this bureaucratic element to the local population that in Twitchell's survey of the area's leading citizens in 1912 most of the Tierra Amarilla entries are either government employees or connected with the area's newspaper, *El Nuevo Estado*.

Coupled with this boom was the overall prosperity affecting American farmers in the years prior to and during World War I. In 1911, the Santa Fe *New Mexican* described Tierra Amarilla as the center of a "great agricultural country" in which the people had "money and plenty of desire to enjoy the comforts of life." To what degree this assessment of prosperity applied to the entire population is unclear, but the architectural evidence suggests that building in Tierra Amarilla continued at a more vigorous pace in the teens than in the nearby villages. Eight homes with shed dormers, a popular stylistic feature during that era, the rosette-windowed Santo Niño church with its large rectory, and finally the current courthouse built in 1915 further attest to the village's vigor during the teens. The result is an architectural variety unique to the area. To make room for this growth, barns and other wooden buildings were often relocated away from the downtown area to the field periphery, suggesting that the village was shifting from agriculture to residential and commercial concerns. This diversification remains apparent, for Tierra Amarilla offers

81. Francisco Luna House, built about 1915.

fewer examples of the traditional Hispanic *casa-corral* arrangement located behind houses.

The Rio Arriba County Courthouse is a significant building remaining from the village's boom period and one symbolizing many of the forces of change in the area. Its Neo-Classical style signifies the presence of a distant state government, a two-day train and buggy ride away, north through Chama and Antonito, Colorado and then south through Española to Santa Fe. It also represents the presence of a legal system that by 1912 had effectively stripped the descendants of the original settlers of their common lands. On the other hand, it has signified an institution providing jobs to a people facing chronic unemployment since the 1920's. Offering these mixed messages, it was the object of the Reies Lopez Tijerina-led courthouse takeover in 1967 in which Tijerina and several followers, having seceded from the United States, seized the building, shot a deputy, took the district judge into custody and proclaimed their intent to redress the wrongs they felt they had suffered in the loss of the land grant properties. Although many of the area residents are quick to condemn the action as impulsive and misdirected, they nevertheless share the frustrations which led to the takeover and maintain ambivalent feelings about outside institutions.

Recent economic decline is more evident in Tierra Amarilla than it is in the other villages and is evidenced in several deserted commercial buildings and a less active ditch association. Ironically, the outside forces which once brought a boom have also brought a more pronounced depression to the village. At first the old gravel highway passed through the village giving rise to the various roadside businesses catering to the passing motorist. Gas stations, garages, a ballroom, bar and cafe complex, and the area's largest motel punctuated the road as it wound through Tierra Amarilla. The old highway was paved in the late 1940's, and then, in the early 1960's, a bypass was constructed. New roadside businesses along the bypass supplanted those in the village. Soon the downtown commerce was virtually dead. Stepped-parapet facades replete with stylized stucco vigas and faded signs, once meant to catch the motorist's eye, are the reminders of that earlier prosperity.

Besides draining the old village center of its commercial vitality, the new highway also bisected many of the area's traditional long, narrow fields. This further decreased the size of many fields which had already been subdivided through inheritance to the point of inefficiency. Modern wheat harvesters simply are not designed for such small fields. The result has been a greater curtailment of farming in Tierra Amarilla than in the other villages where field systems are more intact. Only fifty percent of the irrigated acreage is cultivated, with many fields lying fallow or leased for grazing a few horses or cattle.

This evidence of change contributes to the significance of Tierra Amarilla, for unlike the other villages offering a more uniform example of late nineteenth-century Hispanic settlement patterns, Tierra Amarilla offers an example of those patterns subjected to a greater degree of outside pressure. The presence of the county seat and the region's leading merchant enabled the village to grow and prosper, resulting in some of the finest examples in the state of the incorporation of Anglo-American building elements into local traditions. The passing of that merchant and the new highway bypass have caused an economic decline and loss of some important historic buildings. Nevertheless, most of those important structures and the historic character of the village remain intact.

Tour A: Tierra Amarilla

Mile 0.0 Begin the tour by turning east from US 84 onto NM 162. The partially wooded foothills of the Conejos Mountains, an area heavily logged just after the turn of the century, rise to the east in back of the village.

Mile 0.5 To the right is a federally funded housing project. Its location in a previous-ly irrigated field shows how some recent changes have intruded into earlier land-scape and land use patterns.

82. Rio Arriba County Courthouse, Tierra Amarilla, 1917.

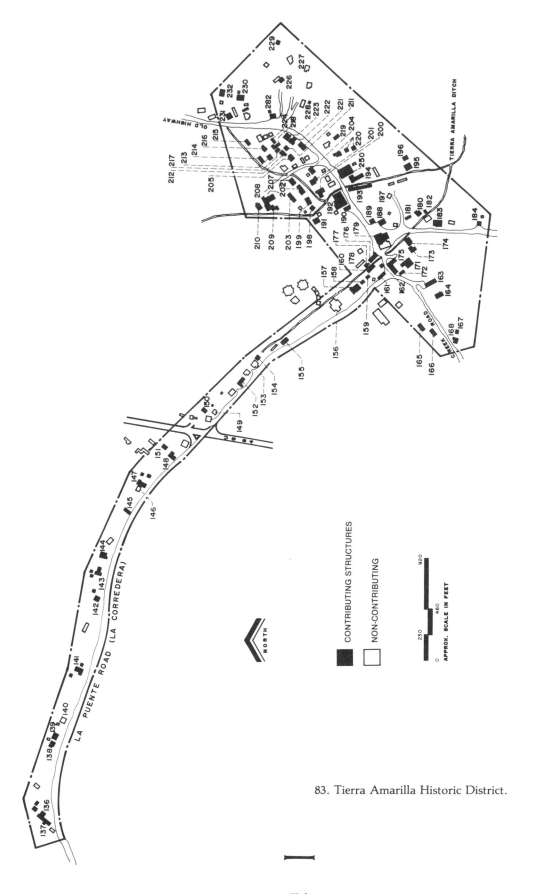

CONTRIBUTING STRUCTURES

NON-CONTRIBUTING

0   230   460   920
APPROX. SCALE IN FEET

NORTH

LA PUENTE ROAD (LA CORREDERA)

OLD HIGHWAY

TIERRA AMARILLA DITCH

CREEK ROAD

83. Tierra Amarilla Historic District.

Mile 0.7 NM 573 leads to the village of Ensenada, two miles north. While not included in the tour, Ensenada does contain a number of historic structures, including houses, barns, and a church individually listed on the National Register of Historic Places.

Mile 0.9 Enter the Tierra Amarilla Historic District. To the right is a good view of the Santo Niño Church, built in 1915. In the foreground runs the high lateral of the Tierra Amarilla Community Ditch. Together, the *acequia,* operated by the ditch association, and the church symbolize two institutions important in local community life.

Mile 1.1 Turn to the right and drive one hundred yards to reach the Santo Niño Church. At twenty yards, on the left, is the Roque Ulibarri House (# 204) a good example of a symmetrical linear house with chamfered porch posts; note also the hipped well house in the front yard. After crossing the lateral of the *acequia,* note building # 207 to the left, one of the few local examples of two-story adobe construction. Just to the east of the church parking lot is the Casados Barn (# 203), part of an elaborate barn-corral complex. It offers a good example of the rough hewn horizontal log construction and dovetailed notching used in many early valley barns. Return to the main road and turn right to continue the tour.

Mile 1.1 On the left side of the road is Lito's Ballroom (# 250), a good example of the Southwest Vernacular style of architecture that characterized commercial roadside buildings in the 1920's and 30's. Note the stepped parapet and the raised ornaments. During the 1950's and 60's the ballroom was a popular dance site and featured well known regional performers such as Al Hurricane. Looking ahead, note the many vacant lots and compare the view with illustration 12, showing the commercial district in its period of prosperity. The vacant lot to the south of the Esquibel Store was once the site of the T.D. Burns Store, the largest mercantile store in the area.

Mile 1.2 Bear to the right at the Tierra Amarilla County Courthouse (# 179), site of the 1967 Tijerina Courthouse raid. Designed by Rapp and Rapp, leading regional architects, and completed in 1917, the building employs the Neo-Classical Style. Facing the courthouse is the Archuleta Store (# 176), a good example of a two-story Folk Territorial Style. The commercial facade in the gable end is uncommon in the area. The date listed in the building's gable is not the actual construction date but one supplied by a movie company using the village as a set.

—

Mile 1.3 On the left, just before the road makes a sharp turn to the right, is the Martinez commercial complex (# 175) with the two story Jose R. Martinez House (# 171) to the rear. The L-shaped commercial structure, built around 1885 in the Territorial Style, served as a store, hotel and saloon. An early area newspaper, *La Voz de Rio Arriba*, was also published here. The house, suggesting the prosperity of its owner, uses a central hall plan. Of note are the many decorative details including the hipped cupola, the chamfered and fluted porch and balcony posts, and the engaged pilasters with molding capitals.

At the sharp turn, off to the left in the Rito de Tierra Amarilla valley, stands the Solomon Luna Barn Complex (# 163 and # 164), furnishing a good example of a barn-corral complex built over an extended period of time (1885-1900) and employing a number of building techniques including adobe, hewn horizontal logs with both double saddle and double box notching, and vertical plank half story walls.

Mile 1.4 The road continues along *La Cordillera*, one of the early spokes of linear settlement radiating from the village along the perimeter of the irrigated fields.

Mile 1.7 The road crosses US 84.

Mile 2.0 The Clara Martinez House (# 143), a good example of an L-shaped house with gable-end balconies, appears to the right. While such balconies occasionally appear in other villages in the upland valleys of New Mexico, nowhere are they as numerous and characteristic of an area's historic housing as they are in La Tierra Amarilla.

84. Manuel and Luis Martinez Houses, built about 1890.

Mile 2.3 The Espiridon and Magdalena Martinez Houses (# 136 and # 137) provide a good example of how houses were sometimes connected as the result of marriage or expanding families. The Tierra Amarilla Historic District ends just beyond this home.

Mile 2.6 On the slope to the right is the *desagüe*, or runoff, of the Tierra Amarilla Community Ditch. Proceed west to begin the La Puente tour at mile 3.5.

Historic Buildings

136 Espiridon Martinez House, N.M. Vernacular, about 1880, significant.

137 Magdalena Martinez House, N.M. Vernacular, about 1880, contributing.

138 Luis Martinez House, illustration 84, N.M. Vernacular, about 1890, contributing.

139 Manuel Martinez House, illustration 84, N.M. Vernacular, about 1890, contributing.

140 Bennie Garcia House, N.M. Vernacular, about 1920, non-contributing.

141 Juan Pablo Samora House, N.M. Vernacular, about 1890, contributing.

142 Benjamin Trujillo House, Hipped Cottage, about 1920, contributing.

143 Clara Martinez House, N.M. Vernacular, about 1890, significant.

144 Raphael Flores House, N.M. Vernacular, about 1895, contributing.

145 Bonifacio Sandoval House, N.M. Vernacular, about 1890, contributing.

146 Eliseo Valdez House, N.M. Vernacular, about 1890, non-contributing.

147 Faustin Martinez House, N.M. Vernacular, about 1890, contributing.

148 Sandra Samora House, N.M. Vernacular, about 1900, contributing.

149 Octaviano Ulibarri House, N.M. Vernacular, about 1900, non-contributing.

150 Ulibarri House, N.M. Vernacular, about 1920, contributing.

151 Anselmo Espinoza House; N.M. Vernacular, about 1890, significant.

152 Tito Ulibarri House, N.M. Vernacular, about 1890, contributing.

153 House, N.M. Vernacular, about 1895, non-contributing.

154 Jeanne Garcia House, Folk Territorial, about 1885, contributing.

155 Rose Romero House, N.M. Vernacular, about 1900, contributing.

156 Chama Valley Board of Education Building, Hipped, about 1925, Former public school building sits on site of original courthouse, contributing.

157 Isaac Garcia House, Folk Territorial, about 1885, contributing.

158 House, N.M. Vernacular, about 1900, contributing.

159 House, N.M. Vernacular, about 1930, contributing.

160 House, N.M. Vernacular, about 1890, contributing.

161 House, N.M. Vernacular, about 1920, contributing.

162 Office Building, Southwest Vernacular, about 1930, contributing.

85. Eluterio Martinez House, built about 1900.

163 Solomon Luna Stock Barn, about 1890, significant.

164 Solomon Luna Hay Barn, N.M. Vernacular, about 1900, significant.

165 Sanchez House, N.M. Vernacular, about 1900, contributing.

166 Clorinda Sanchez Brown House, N.M. Vernacular, about 1900, contributing.

#167 Herrera Outbuilding, N.M. Vernacular, about 1890, contributing.

168 Herrera House, N.M Vernacular, about 1900, contributing.

171 Jose R. Martinez House, illustrations 10, 28, Territorial, pre-1885, significant.

172 Shed, N.M. Vernacular, about 1890, 1920, contributing.

173 Adela Casias House, N.M. Vernacular, about 1890, contributing.

174 Evaraldo Casias House, N.M. Verncular, about 1920, contributing.

175 Jose R. Martinez Building, illustration 47, Territorial, about 1885, significant. Important as commercial building, saloon and hotel; local newspaper *La Voz de Rio Arriba* was published here.

176 Archuleta Store, illustration 52, Folk Territorial, about 1880, significant, Building used as movie setting in 1970's.

177 Rosina Archuleta House, N.M. Vernacular, about 1890, contributing.

178 Storage Compound Ruins, N.M. Vernacular, about 1900, non-contributing.

179 Rio Arriba County Courthouse, illustration 82, Neo-Classical; 1915, significant. Classic interior processional space through heavy arches and up broad staircase to lobby; split switchback stairs lead to Roman windows over landing and switchback up unified stair to court chambers.

#180 Santiago Romero House, illustration 86, N.M. Vernacular, about 1890, contributing.

181 House, N.M. Vernacular, about 1910, contributing.

182 Johnny Martinez House, N.M. Vernacular, about 1930, contributing.

183 Julio Martinez Service Station, Highway-Wood Vernacular, about 1930, contributing.

184 Joe Sanchez Service Station, Southwest Vernacular, about 1930, contributing.

188 Eluterio Martinez House, illustration 85, Folk Territorial, about 1900, significant.

189 William Kinderman-Donato Sanchez House, Folk Territorial, about 1900, significant. The ruins of a pool hall and saloon lie to the north.

190 Frank Esquibel Garage, Hipped Cottage, about 1930, contributing.

191 Frank Esquibel House, illustration 31, N.M. Vernacular, about 1900, contributing.

192 Valley Theater and Esquibel Market, N.M. Vernacular, about 1935, contributing. Theatre interior a central open space with horse-shoe arranged wood auditorium seats; 20' wide stage; balcony with projection room.

193 Greenleaf Cabins, Southwest Vernacular, about 1930, contributing.

194 Solomon Luna House, N.M. Vernacular, about 1885, significant.

195 Francisco Luna II House, illustration 81, Free Classic, about 1915, significant.

196 Francisco Luna II Barn, tree ring dated 1893, significant. Previously located on hill near present day water towers but moved when # 195 was built around 1915.

197 Tony Olivas House, Hipped-N.M. Vernacular, about 1915, noncontributing.

198 Cirilo DeVargas House, N.M. Vernacular, about 1900, contributing.

199 Gumercindo DeVargas House, N.M Vernacular, about 1900, contributing.

86. Santiago Romero House, built about 1890.

200 Pedro Gomez House, N.M. Vernacular, about 1890; 1917 addition, east-facing with two stories, significant. Portion built in 1917 served as weekly hotel for school children from outlying districts.

201 Antonio Casados House, N.M. Vernacular, about 1900, contributing.

202 Roque Ulibarri House, N.M. Vernacular, about 1880-1900, significant.

203 Casados Barn, about 1880, significant.

204 House, N.M. Vernacular, about 1900, significant.

205 Benito Sandoval House, N.M. Vernacular, about 1900, contributing.

206 Frank X. Martinez House, N.M. Vernacular, about 1910, non-contributing.

207 Lucas Martinez House, N.M. Vernacular, 1914-15, significant.

208 Santo Niño Church, illustration 78, N.M. Vernacular-Gothic Revival, 1915, cruciform plan, significant.

209 Santo Niño Rectory, N.M. Vernacular, about 1907, significant.

210 Santo Niño Storage Building, about 1900, contributing.

211 House, N.M. Vernacular, about 1920, contributing.

212 P. Martinez House, N.M. Vernacular, about 1900, contributing.

213 Garage, N.M. Vernacular, about 1920, contributing.

214 Perfecto Samora House, N.M. Vernacular, about 1910, contributing.

215 Josefa Trujillo House, N.M. Vernacular, about 1910, contributing.

216 Atencio Barn, about 1890, contributing.

217 House, N.M. Vernacular, about 1920, contributing.

218 Atencio House, N.M. Vernacular, about 1910, contributing.

219 Atocha Esquibel House; N.M. Vernacular, about 1910, contributing.

220 Eliseo Esquibel House, N.M. Vernacular, about 1900, significant.

221 Juan Lopez House, N.M. Vernacular, about 1900, contributing.

222 Mickey Jaramillo House, N.M. Vernacular, about 1900, contributing.

223 Bernabe Martinez House, Hipped Cottage/N.M. Vernacular, about 1920, contributing.

224 Arturo Atencio House, N.M. Vernacular, about 1930, contributing.

225 Salvador Samora House, N.M. Vernacular, about 1930, non-contributing.

226 Storage Building, N.M. Vernacular, about 1900, contributing.

227 House, N.M. Vernacular, about 1920, contributing.

228 Julia Lovato House, N.M. Vernacular, about 1910, contributing.

229 Luna Barn, N.M. Vernacular, about 1880, significant. Moved to present site from site of magistrate's office.

230 Juanita Garcia House, N.M. Vernacular, about 1910, contributing.

231 Juan Martinez Jr. House, N.M. Vernacular, about 1912, contributing.

232 Juan Martinez Jr. Barn, N.M. Vernacular, about 1900, contributing.

250 Lito's Ballroom, illustration 53, Southwest Vernacular; about 1925; contributing. Building housed a cafe, bar, dancehall and store. Popular dance site into 1960's.

6 — La Puente

*E*stablished in 1860 or 1861, the village of La Puente is one of the best-preserved examples of a linear village — the most common village type of Hispanic settlement in New Mexico in the nineteenth century. Although the houses respond to Anglo-American attitudes by being free-standing, set back from and facing the street with ornamented porches, they are built of traditional Hispanic materials and most are composed of long files of self-contained rooms. The private courtyard spaces defined by the houses, barns and fences also continue the Hispanic tradition of combining the house and farm buildings in one unit, sometimes called the *casa-corral*. Among the outbuildings are some of the most outstanding and best-preserved examples of Hispanic barns in New Mexico.

The La Puente Historic District covers an area of approximately eighteen acres and includes twenty-five houses, six barns, another six outbuildings, one store and a church. Of the houses, twelve were built between 1870 and 1895, eleven between 1895 and 1920, one between 1920 and 1940, and three since 1940. The houses were built of adobe, horizontal log, *jacal* and railroad ties, covered with stucco and topped by corrugated metal gables, or in one case, a hipped roof. They stand thirty to fifty feet from the road; behind them another thirty to sixty feet, situated against the

87. San Miguel Church, built 1912-1914.

back fence line, are the barns and outbuildings built of horizontal logs or railroad ties and topped by corrugated metal gables.

Tour B: La Puente

Drive west from Highway 84/64 at either the Los Ojos or the south Tierra Amarilla turn off, in the direction of El Vado Lake, approximately 1.5 miles to the intersection of State Roads 112 and 531. Begin the tour here by driving west on NM 531.

Mile 0.35 As the road begins its descent, the view to the right overlooks the long, narrow La Puente fields which lie on the middle plateau. Below, at the base of the hill, a growth of willows marks the main irrigation ditch while lateral ditches run from right to left at approximately one-third and two-thirds of the way across the fields. As a result of subdivision through inheritance, these fields range in width from one hundred yards (possibly an original undivided field) to as narrow as twenty feet.

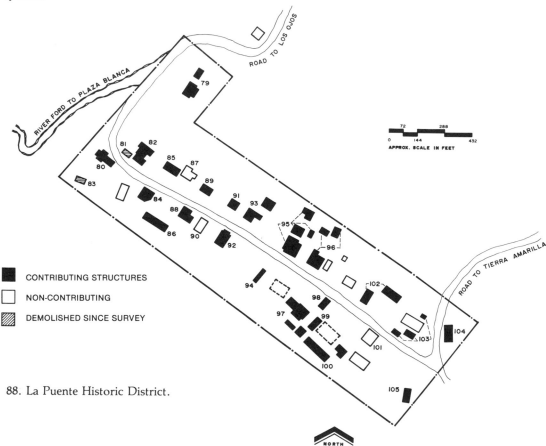

88. La Puente Historic District.

Mile 0.7 To the right, the linear plan of La Puente set between fields is clearly visible. The barns and sheds in a straight line at the edge of the village, combine with the houses beyond to form a set of farm corral complexes. On the opposite side of the road, the pattern is repeated.

Mile 0.8 The road parallels the irrigation ditch on the right, with its thick growth of willow, before turning right into La Puente.

Mile 0.9 To the right, stands the Rose Valdez House (# 103) built between 1890 and 1910 with an original room of *jacal* to the left, and an addition of railroad ties to the right. To the left of the road, behind building # 101, is the Gumercindo Salazar House, built during the 1980s. It combines a ranch style first floor plan with a traditional second story design. The next building at the street's edge on the left was a store and post office during the 1930s.

Mile 1.0 The Carlos Manzanares House (# 96), on the right, built about 1910, is a fine Hipped Cottage with Queen Anne Style details on the porch. A bit further on the left, House # 94 combines an original room of hewn horizontal logs with a later addition of vertical planks, wooden lath and earthen plaster. A small *contra acequia* cuts in front of this house.

89. Carlos Manzanares House, built about 1910.

90. Barn, built about 1890.

Mile 1.1 Road crosses a *contra acequia,* and immediately on the left, is an L-shaped house with a well house in the frontyard. Just beyond on the left is one of the finest Hispanic log barns in the state (# 86). It has three separate cribs of hewn horizontal logs with double box notching. The cribs are connected with cross beams and vertical plank walls at the rear. House # 85 on the right provides a good example of an exterior stairs under an extended gable roof. Directly ahead is the San Miguel Church at the most prominent location in the village. Its front stucco is scored in imitation of stone block construction.

Mile 1.2 Road curves to the right, and two hundred feet on the left, the river ford road to Plaza Blanca descends to the Chama River. Beyond the river lined with cottonwoods, the Plaza Blanca fields stretch up to the village perched on a hill above the irrigation ditch. Another two hundred feet and the La Puente Historic District ends.

The tour ends here, although this road can be taken north approximately 3 miles to Los Ojos. The road dips to the Chama River *bosque* (cottonwood forest), which is occasionally impassable after rains, before joining the Hatchery Road Spur of the Los Ojos tour (see page 95).

79 House, N.M. Vernacular, about 1900, contributing.

80 San Miguel Church; illustration 87; N.M. Vernacular, 1912-14; cruciform plan; adobe, stucco scored on facade to resemble stone blocks; significant. Original interior — tongue-and-groove wainscot, plaster walls and ornamental pressed metal ceiling — now covered by wood paneling.

81 Tircio Gonzales House, N.M. Vernacular, about 1890, demolished.

82 Willie Trujillo House, N.M. Vernacular, about 1880, significant.

83 House, N.M. Vernacular, tree ring date 1916, demolished.

84 Christina Lincoln House, N.M. Vernacular, about 1910; contributing.

85 House, N.M. Vernacular, about 1890; contributing.

86 Barn, illustration 90; tree ring date 1901; 3 one-story modules of hewn horizontal logs with double box notching; significant.

87 House, N.M. Vernacular, about 1890, non-contributing.

88 House, N.M. Vernacular, about 1900, contributing.

89 House, illustration 18, N.M. Vernacular, about 1885, contributing.

90 Belarmino Lopez House, N.M. Vernacular, about 1900, non-contributing.

91 Cruz Cordova House, N.M. Vernacular, about 1900, contributing.

92 Frank Manzanares House, illustration 91, N.M. Vernacular/Bungalow, about 1930, contributing.

93 Martinez House, N.M. Vernacular, about 1890, contributing.

91. Frank Manzanares House, built about 1930.

94 House, N.M. Vernacular, about 1890/1920, contributing.

95 Ruben Manzanares House, N.M. Vernacular/Southwest Vernacular porch, house about 1920/porch about 1935, significant.

96 Carlos Manzanares House, illustration 89, Hipped Cottage/N.M. Vernacular, about 1910, significant. Barn about 35 feet northeast (significant): hewn horizontal log with double box notch, horizontal plank half-story wall, about 1890.

97 Alfredo Ulibarri House, Territorial Style/N.M. Vernacular, about 1885; significant.

98 Old Post Office, Southwest Vernacular, about 1930, contributing.

99 Ulibarri House/storage, illustration 15, about 1895, significant.

100 Gumercindo Salazar Barn, illustrations 44-46, log cribs and tree ring date to 1897 and 1898, significant.

101 Gumercindo Salazar House, N.M. Vernacular, about 1900, noncontributing.

102 Trujillo House, illustration 72, N.M. Vernacular, 1912, contributing.

103 Jose Valdez House, N.M. Vernacular, about 1890/1910, contributing.

104 Eudan Ulibarri House, N.M. Vernacular, about 1915, contributing.

105 Trujillo-Archuleta House, N.M. Vernacular, about 1885+, contributing.

7 — Los Ojos

From its founding in 1860, Los Ojos was one of the two major settlements in the area; the other was nearby Tierra Amarilla, the county seat. While Los Ojos began as a farming village, it also quickly developed into a commercial center for nearby Hispanic farmers and the Jicarilla Apaches to the west. In addition, it became a center for religious and educational activities, with the area's main church and a convent school. Evidence of these various roles is well preserved in the historic stores, warehouses and church. The Historic District covers approximately sixty-six acres.

The village's houses include some of the best-preserved examples of the local folk architecture which incorporated Anglo-American elements such as gabled roofs and jig-saw ornament into the basic Hispanic tradition of adobe and log construction, and single-file or L-shaped plans. The most distinctive local elements — a half-story wall, raising the roof to a comfortable level, and gable balconies — fuse the two traditions in an innovative way. Of the structures erected before 1940, forty-one are houses (one of which was converted from a school), nine commercial buildings, ten farm outbuildings and one a church. Thirty of these were built between 1870 and 1900, fifteen between 1900 and 1920, another fifteen between 1920 and 1940, and eighteen new buildings since 1940.

Los Ojos is also one of the best remaining examples of the linear or roadside settlement pattern, which typified most nineteenth century Hispanic villages in New Mex-

92. Los Ojos from the southeast.

—

93. St. Joseph's Church and Convent School (now demolished).

ico. Buildings are arranged one or two deep on either side of the major roads. In the commercial area near the turn in the Old Highway, they stand side by side at the street's edge. In the more rural portions of the village to the north and south, they are set back as much as one-hundred feet.

The name Los Ojos came originally from the springs one mile south of the village, where the state fish hatchery now stands. *Los Ojos* means the eyes, but in New Mexico Spanish, it also means the springs. The name Parkview was transferred to the village in the early 1880s from a speculative town to the north, which had failed, but which had a post office that moved with the name. After a historian from the village, Robert Torrez, who was then a student at Highlands University, uncovered this history, a petition drive was started to get the original name back. In 1972, the Rio Arriba County Commission renamed the village, Los Ojos.

Tour C: Los Ojos

This tour begins at the intersection of Highway 84/64 and N.M. 112. From the intersection, head north on the old highway to Los Ojos, not west toward El Vado Lake.

Mile 0.1 The road crosses the *desagüe* (discharge) of the Ensenada ditch, where excess water flows off the upper plateau on its way to join the Parkview ditch and the springs at the fish hatchery, which together supply the La Puente ditch to the south.

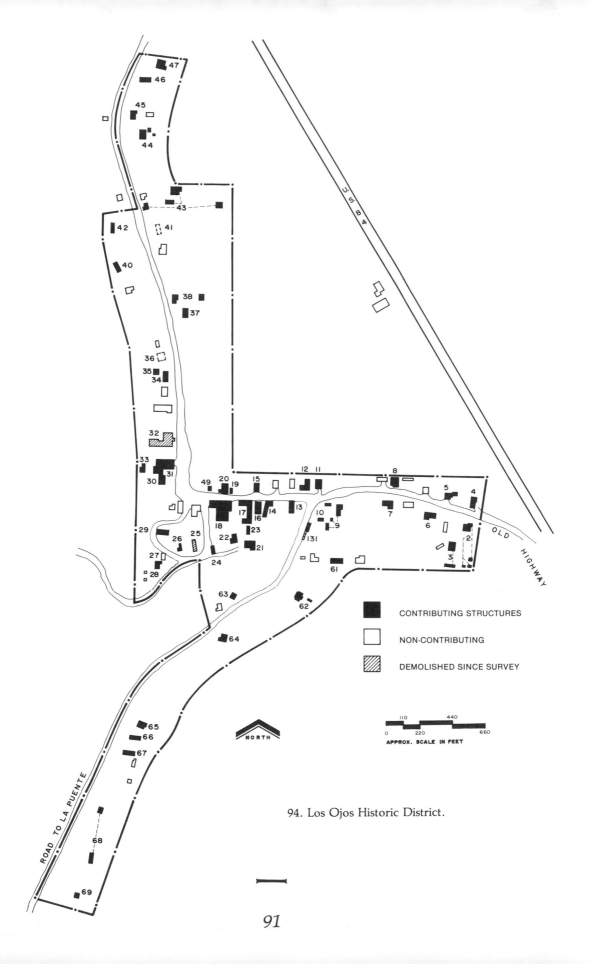

94. Los Ojos Historic District.

CONTRIBUTING STRUCTURES

NON-CONTRIBUTING

DEMOLISHED SINCE SURVEY

APPROX. SCALE IN FEET

NORTH

U.S. 84

OLD HIGHWAY

ROAD TO LA PUENTE

Mile 0.35 The pull off to the left offers an excellent view of the long, narrow fields and the T-shaped, linear plan of Los Ojos. At the head of the main road stands St. Joseph's Church; beyond it, the middle plateau of Los Ojos drops to the Chama River valley. Along the edge of the road, here, are a few remaining ponderosa pine which were once numerous on the plateau below.

Mile 0.4 To the right, Our Lady of Lourdes Grotto was built between 1915 and 1919 to commemorate Josepha Burn's escape from mishap when she lost control of her buggy and the horse raced down the steep road, an escape which she attributed to divine intervention. In this deeply religious community, all those who live in or enter the valley come under the protection of the Virgin of the shrine. Although the authors are secular Protestants, we unconsciously responded to the importance of this site by beginning our survey of the cultural resources of the area here.

To the north, the early 1960s highway by-pass can be seen cutting through the long Los Ojos fields.

Mile 0.5 The road swings left over the Park View ditch and into the Los Ojos Historic District. The division between the arid hillside of chamisa and thistle above the ditch and the moist cultivated fields below is particularly clear here.

Mile 0.75 On the left, the Mercure-Abeyta House (#7), built about 1880, is a particularly fine example of the distinctive local building type which combines traditional Hispanic adobe construction and linear plans with second story bedrooms and Queen Anne style details on the long porch and gable balcony.

Mile 0.8 The turn left begins the Fish Hatchery Road Spur tour (see page 95). The Archuleta and Valdez Houses (# 12 and # 13), on opposite sides of the road, besides being well detailed examples of the local house type, both have well houses. The high water table, five to fifteen feet below the surface throughout most of the villages, was easily tapped for drinking water.

Mile 0.85 The Park View Super Market on the left (# 16) was built of adobe about 1890, and its false front of faintly-Classical, pressed metal was added about 1910. The Los Ganados del Valle economic development cooperative purchased the building late in 1988 and plans to develop it as a feed and supply, and general store. It will also house a coffee shop and bakery, and serve as a retail outlet for local family businesses.

95. North of the church, Los Ojos.

From here to the turn in the road, several buildings have wall murals: "Settlement of La Tierra Amarilla" painted by Brooks Willis about 1935 (building # 17), an old road map and Apache blanket patterns on the Burns Store (# 18) and a number of other murals from the 1988 Summer Art program.

Mile 0.9 On the left, T.D. Burns began his mercantile business in the 1860s on this site, although most of the current building (# 16) probably dates to the 1880s (illustration 77). Since 1983, Los Ganados del Valle has renovated the building for the Tierra Wools showroom, weaving room, wool washing and storage, and offices.

Mile 0.95 The road curves to the right in front of St. Joseph's Catholic Church, built of adobe in 1935 and 1936 on the site of the first, 1880s church. The rectory, attached to the south of the church, and the two story church school, which once stood to the north, made this an important educational and religious center for the area.

Mile 1.0 The Francisco Salazar House (# 34) on the left, built about 1900, has a wrap-around porch, two interior stairs, and a gable balcony with a jig-sawn railing.

Mile 1.3 On the right is a large barn (# 46) with two log cribs; one, beside the road, is of round, unhewn logs with saddle notching, the other, of hewn logs with double box notching. The hayloft is formed, like the second floors of many area houses, by raising the roof on a three-foot-high wall of horizontal planks.

Mile 1.35 End of the Los Ojos Historic District.

Mile 1.45 Turn left (north) on Highway 84/64.

Mile 1.5 Tour E, Plaza Blanca, begins here to the left.

Mile 1.65 Approximately seventy-five yards to the left (west) is the Casados House, one of a half dozen, two story houses built during the 1880s by Hispanic merchants and ranchers. Its center hall plan and Territorial style detailing represent the adoption of Anglo-American style on the grandest scale affordable.

Mile 1.7 On the left, the Sanchez-March House, build about 1880, combines modular, adobe construction with the plan of the officers' quarters at Fort Lowell. Lathe-turned and cut-out wooden detailing adorn the wrap-around porch, while finials crest the roof.

Mile 1.9 Another house patterned on the Fort Lowell officers' quarters stands deteriorating on the left.

The tour ends here. Proceed north approximately one half mile to Los Brazos (Tour D), or return to the Plaza Blanca Tour or Hatchery Road Spur Tour.

96. Parkview Fish Hatchery, south of Los Ojos, built 1932-34.

Fish Hatchery Road Spur Tour

This route follows the brow of the middle plateau, just above the flood plain of the Rio Chama. This dirt road leads south at Mile 0.8 of the Los Ojos Tour to the State Fish Hatchery, then beside a number of historic buildings and finally to the village of La Puente.

Mile 0.1 To the left is the Lopez-Martinez House (# 62), an excellent example of an adobe Hipped Cottage with a symmetrical facade. It combines Territorial style pedimented lintels over the windows with Queen Anne style porch details — a spindle railing, slender, lathe-turned columns and cut-out brackets.

Mile 0.2 This point offers a good view to the right (northwest) of the defensible point upon which the early settlers first built. In the foreground, a dirt road follows the edge of the bluff down to irrigated fields which stretch west to the Chama River.

Mile 0.5 Los Ojos Historic District ends.

Mile 0.7 To the left is the Teodoro Martinez House (# 70) a good example of the local story-and-a-half building form with a door in the gable. The wrap-around porch on three sides protecting ninety per cent of the exterior walls attests to the average annual sixty-five inches of snowfall.

Mile 0.8 To the left three tenths of a mile is the state's Parkview Fish Hatchery, built between 1932 and 1934. The formal arrangement of the structures and the symmetrical building facades are typical of 1920s and 1930s Beaux Arts architectural design. (This formal arrangement was undermined in 1988 when portions of the approach ramps and the garages to the left, which balanced the office building to the right, were removed). The building's rough-faced masonry, and exposed rafters and purlins resemble many other 1930s government recreation structures, a building style which might be characterized as "WPA Rustic." The springs (Los Ojos in New Mexican Spanish) to the rear provide waters for the hatchery. From the hatchery, the water is added to the discharge from the Park View and Ensenada ditches to supply the La Puente Ditch which runs to the south.

Mile 0.9 To the left is the Transito Martinez barn which has been tree ring dated to 1911. Its hewn logs, double box notching and raised hayloft are typical of local barns.

— ▬ —

Mile 1.0 To the left, the George Becker house and farm-ranch complex is one of the finest in the valley. The house was built in 1918 and 1919 for Denver businessman George Becker and his wife Emma, daughter of the area's leading merchant, T.D. Burns. It is among the most elaborate Bungalows in New Mexico with its picturesque composition of intersecting gables and gabled oriels, its half-timbering, "cut-out" facia boards, and exposed rafters and brackets. The river-cobble retaining walls and grove of aspens are unlike any other historic landscaping in the area. To the rear is a large log barn with a gambrel roof; to the right (south) is a 1938 Southwest Vernacular bunk house, and further to the south is a log house (# 109) with dovetail notching and an unusually steep roof.

Mile 1.2 To the left is a house known locally as the Officer's House, which probably dates to the 1870s. Its plan is based on the officers' quarters of Camp Plummer/Fort Lowell which was located in the fields east of this house during the late 1860s.

The Fish Hatchery Road tour ends here. The route can be retraced to rejoin the Los Ojos tour, or you can continue south. That route, which dips to the flood plain of the Chama before arriving at La Puente (Mile 3), is generally good, although after rains, it can become muddy and impassable.

97. The Officer's House, south of Los Ojos, built about 1870-75.

96

Historic Buildings

2   Antonio Lente House, illustration 32, N.M. Vernacular, about 1900, two-story, L-shaped plan, significant.

3   Vialpondo House, N.M. Vernacular, about 1905, contributing.

4   Sanchez House, N.M. Vernacular, interior jacal wall, tree ring date 1898, contributing.

5   House, N.M. Vernacular, about 1905, contributing.

6   Ortiz House, N.M. Vernacular, about 1880/1895, contributing.

7   Mercure-Valdez-Abeyta House, Folk Territorial, about 1880, significant.

8   Public Health Building, Bungalow, 1934, contributing.

9   Old School-Torrez House, N.M. Vernacular, about 1890, contributing.

10   Service station and cabins, Southwest Vernacular, about 1930, contributing.

11   Samora House, N.M. Vernacular/Territorial, about 1875/1965, contributing.

12   Archuleta House, illustration 48, Folk Territorial, about 1890, significant.

13   Valdez House, illustrations 23, 24, 98, Folk Territorial; begun about 1865, significant.

14   Quintana House, Folk Territorial, 1875/1885, significant.

15   M & M Store, Southwest Vernacular, about 1935, contributing.

16   Park View Super Market, illustration 51, N.M. Vernacular/faintly Classical facade, about 1890/facade about 1910, significant.

17   T.D. Burns Warehouse, N.M. Vernacular, about 1890. Large eaves overhang at front shields mural, "Settlement of La Tierra Amarilla," by Brooks Willis, about 1935. Substantial remodeling about 1984.

98. Valdez House, porch added about 1885.

18   T.D. Burns Store; illustrations 76, 77; N.M. Vernacular; about 1880/1900; Leading commercial and social center used variously for: T.D. Burns Store (area's leading mercantile store, 1870-1930s), Wheeler's Hardware and General Store (1950s-1960s), Tierra Wools (weaving cooperative work and showrooms, 1980s); Post Office; Indian souvenirs; automobile garage, dances, and so forth. Significant structure.

19   Frontier Bar, Southwest Vernacular, about 1930, contributing.

20   Sanchez Store, Southwest Vernacular, about 1935, contributing.

21   Serrano House, N.M. Vernacular, about 1885, contributing.

22   House, N.M. Vernacular, about 1880, contributing.

23   House, N.M. Vernacular, about 1910, contributing.

24   House, N.M. Vernacular, about 1910, contributing.

25 Rascon House, illustrations 21, 22, N.M. Vernacular, about 1885/1920, demolished about 1985.

26 House, N.M. Vernacular, about 1920, contributing.

27 House, N.M. Vernacular, 1900/1970, non-contributing.

28 Martinez House, N.M. Vernacular, about 1880/1900, contributing.

29 Drake House, N.M. Vernacular, about 1890, contributing.

30 St. Joseph's Church Rectory, Bungalow, 1935, contributing.

31 St. Joseph's Catholic Church, illustration 93, Gothic Revival, 1935-36, significant.

32 St. Joseph's Convent School; illustration 93, N.M. Vernacular, 1923, demolished about 1987.

33 House, N.M. Vernacular, contributing.

34 Fernando Salazar House, illustration 38, N.M. Vernacular/Folk Territorial, about 1900, significant.

35 House, N.M. Vernacular, about 1910, contributing.

36 Casados House, illustration 68, Territorial Style, about 1885, non-contributing.

37 Martinez-Rhodes House, N.M. Vernacular, about 1900, contributing.

38 Francis Salazar House, N.M. Vernacular, about 1890, significant.

40 House, N.M. Vernacular, about 1890, contributing.

41 Martinez House, N.M. Vernacular, about 1935, non-contributing.

42 Frank Abeyta House, N.M. Vernacular, about 1890, significant.

43 Torrez Phillips 66 Station, Southwest Vernacular, about 1930, contributing.

44 Salazar House, N.M. Vernacular, 1925, significant.

45 Praxcedes Salazar House, Territorial Style/N.M. Vernacular, about 1890, significant.

46 Barn, illustration 43, about 1890, significant.

47 Suazo House, N.M. Vernacular, about 1910, adobe, contributing.

49 Service Station, Southwest Vernacular, about 1935, contributing.

61 House, N.M. Vernacular, about 1930, contributing.

62 Lopez-Martinez House, illustration 30, Hipped Cottage, 1885/1905, significant.

63 Barn, about 1920, contributing.

64 House, N.M. Vernacular, about 1880, contributing.

65 Esquibel House, Hipped Cottage/N.M. Vernacular, about 1905, significant.

66 House, N.M. Vernacular, about 1885, contributing.

67 House, N.M. Vernacular, about 1885, contributing.

68 Gilbert Martinez House, N.M. Vernacular, about 1890, significant.

69 House, N.M. Vernacular, 1903, earthen plaster over jacal, contributing. A one-room honeymoon house.

133 Torrez Barn, two hewn horizontal log rectangles (on different levels), gabled roof removed about 1978, one portion demolished about 1985, contributing.

8 — Los Brazos

*E*stablished in 1860 and 1861, Los Brazos is one of the best-preserved historic farming villages in New Mexico. It contains many of the finest examples of a regional folk architectural type, which innovatively combines a Hispanic tradition with some Anglo-American elements. Typical features such as adobe and log construction, and the accretion of one-room modules were augmented by corrugated roofing and mass-produced doors, windows, ornamental posts and cut-out brackets, and innovations such as the half-story wall and the gable balcony. The Los Brazos Historic District covers an area of approximately thirty-two acres and includes twenty-five houses (one of which is a converted store), a school house and eleven farm buildings. Of the houses, twelve were built between 1875 and 1900, eight between 1900 and 1915, two between 1915 and 1940 and four since 1940. The village's fields lie to the west, irrigated by the El Barranco ditch, and to the south along the Rio Brazos.

Tour D: Los Brazos

From Highway 84/64, just north of the Rio Brazos, take the turn off to the northeast into Los Brazos. This is the route of the old highway.

On the hill to the left, entering the village, the Bernardo Sanchez House (# 127) was restored about 1985, including the reconstruction of the porch based on historic photographs. Oral tradition holds that the first *fuertes* (stronghold houses) were built north of the Sanchez House, near the edge of the hill.

99. Los Brazos from the north.

CONTRIBUTING STRUCTURES

NON-CONTRIBUTING

NORTH

APPROX. SCALE IN FEET

100. Los Brazos Historic District.

101. Martinez and Trujillo Houses.

Park in Los Brazos where the dirt road forks to the right in front of the old school (# 110).

Walk east on the dirt road approximately seventy yards past the school, for a view to the south of the Abeyta family complex. The three houses (#s 112, 113, 128), built from 1880 to 1900, form a partial courtyard. The Marianita Abeyta Quintana House (# 128), on the left, in its current weathered condition, shows the sequence of construction: a one room *jacal* on the right, a larger, story-and-a-half, adobe addition to the left, and horizontal log infill above the *jacal*. To the right, behind the Jose Abeyta House (# 113), a storage building of hewn horizontal logs with double box notching may have been the original house.

Return to the school and follow the paved highway north through the village.

102. Emiliano and Narcisco Martinez House, built 1870s.

Approximately one hundred yards northwest of the school, House # 123 was built in the 1870s by brothers Emiliano and Narcisco Martinez. The slight change in the roof level marks the division between the brothers' separate sections. This division is also indicated by different window lintels and molding "capitals" on the porch posts.

To the left of the highway, approximately one hundred yards north of the school, the Trujillo House (# 122), probably built in the 1880s, has a gable balcony and a Territorial style porch wrapping the inside of its U-shape.

The next two buildings on the left to the north were built between 1865 and 1912 by Fernando Martinez and his family (see pages 31-32). The larger of the two (# 119), with Territorial style details, was built in at least three stages. In 1987, it was refurbished into a bed and breakfast inn by a Martinez descendant and her husband. The building to the left (# 121), with stock classical columns, was built in 1910. It originally had double doors under the gable balcony which led to a store on the first floor with a residence above. These buildings follow the Hispanic tradition of linear additions and form an informal courtyard space. But rather than completely enclose the courtyard, as would have been done a hundred years before in Abiquiu or in Santa Fe, the Martinez family chose to build a second story and to orient their buildings toward the road in Anglo-American fashion.

Beyond and behind the Martinez complex is the Valdez House (# 120), built around the turn of the century with a gable end stairway.

103. Rear of Fernando Martinez House and Store/House.

104. Fermin Martinez House, built about 1890, now demolished.

Historic Buildings

110 Old County School House, N.M. Vernacular, pre-1911, significant. Double Folk Territorial doors removed about 1980.

111 Gallegos House, illustration 105, N.M. Vernacular, about 1900, contributing.

112 Old Abeyta House, Territorial Style/N.M. Vernacular, 1881-90, significant.

113 Jose Abeyta House, N.M. Vernacular, about 1890, contributing. Shed/original house, about 15 feet northwest, about 1880, significant.

105. Gallegos House, built about 1900, addition about 1930.

114 House, N.M. Vernacular, about 1910, contributing.

115 Fermin Martinez House, about 1890, in ruins, 1988.

116 House, N.M. Vernacular, about 1910, contributing.

117 Gallegos House, N.M. Vernacular, about 1925, contributing. Barn about 35 feet east (contributing), hewn horizontal log with dovetail notching and vertical plank, log section tree ring date 1907.

118 Abeyta House, illustration 106, N.M. Vernacular, about 1900, significant.

119 Fernando Martinez Houses, illustrations 39-41, 103, Territorial Style/N.M. Vernacular, about 1865, significant.

120 Valdez House, illustration 37, N.M. Vernacular, about 1895, contributing.

121 Fernando Martinez Store/House, illustrations 14, 49, Folk Territorial; about 1900, significant.

122 Rita Trujillo House, Folk Territorial, about 1880, significant. Two-room house connected to west side, about 1900, contributing.

123 Emiliano and Narcisco Martinez Houses, illustration 102, Territorial Style, 1870-1880, significant.

124 House, N.M. Vernacular, about 1920, contributing.

125 House, N.M. Vernacular, about 1890, non-contributing

126 House, N.M. Vernacular, about 1890-1905, significant.

127 Bernardo Sanchez House, Territorial Style, about 1875-1885, contributing. Porch reconstructed based on historic photo, about 1985.

128 Marianita Abeyta Quintana House, N.M. Vernacular, about 1895, contributing.

129 House, N.M. Vernacular, about 1910, contributing.

130 House, N.M. Vernacular, about 1890, contributing.

132 House, about 1900, non-contributing.

106. Abeyta House, built about 1900.

9 — *Plaza Blanca*

Settled in the mid-1870s, the village of Plaza Blanca is one of the best preserved examples of a nineteenth-century Hispanic village in New Mexico. Because of its limited field area and its separation from the other villages of La Tierra Amarilla, which lie to the east of the Chama River, it developed on a modest scale, realizing the essentials of Hispanic architecture and settlements with little elaboration or evident Anglo-American influence. The most basic construction material — *jacal* with earthen plaster — predominates. The traditional arrangement of self-contained rooms in a single file plan accounts for all but two of the houses, which employ the next simplest variation, the L-shaped plan. These houses line the high side of the village's single road, forming an uncomplicated example of the typical nineteenth-century linear settlement pattern. Perpendicular to the road, traditional long lots extend up from the Chama River to the sandy hills behind town. Most properties repeat a fundamental Hispanic organization of space: first the river, then the fields, above them the *acequia*, the road, the houses and finally above and behind them are the corrals formed by barns, sheds and fences.

The Plaza Blanca Historic District covers an area of approximately nineteen acres and includes ten houses, a church or *capilla* which is a converted school, and six outbuildings, including three sheds and corral complexes. Of the houses, nine were built between 1880 and 1910, and one since 1930. The church was built in 1920. The outbuildings predate 1940. Only two of the houses have the half-story construction more frequently found in the other villages. Further evidence of the modest nature of these structures is the lack of wood detailing. Porch supports are simply log post, and in six of the houses adobe plaster rather than hard stucco covers the building.

The expansive plateaus and fields of Los Ojos, Ensenada, and Tierra Amarilla are not duplicated here on the west bank. The topography limits Plaza Blanca to an *acequia* system feeding a smaller area of rectangular fenced fields, much like those found in narrower mountain valleys common elsewhere in northern New Mexico. Yet as one approaches this *acequia*, the contrasts common to all ditch-fed areas become apparent. Below the *acequia* lush grasses and flowers thrive in the moist soil. Above the *acequia* a sunbleached dryness dominates with seasonal vegetation surviving only because of its modest moisture requirements. So striking is this contrast that, both in aerial photographs and from the hilltop in back of the village, the *acequia* appears not as a ribbon of water but as a strand of vegetation.

The farm implement graveyard on the hill above Plaza Blanca signifies the shift from horse to gasoline power and the abandonment of grain crops. Horse or small

107. Plaza Blanca from the west.

tractor-drawn and relatively small and lightweight, these early thrashers, rakes and reapers permitted access to the small narrow fields with their ditch laterals without disturbing the delicate *acequia* and fence system. In contrast, modern gas-powered combines introduced in the 1930s and 1940s are more expensive and impractical in such small scale conditions and have effectively eliminated the earlier more diverse range of crops, particularly wheat and barley. Unused reminders of an earlier era, the implements and field landscape complement the village architecture — evoking a past that has largely disappeared along the more travelled roads of the state.

Tour E: Plaza Blanca

The tour begins at the intersection of Highway 84/64 and state road 95, between Los Ojos and Los Brazos (see illustration 79). Proceed west on Road 95 (the signs will say "To Heron Lake") for views of the Chama Valley and Los Ojos, and a tour of the village of Plaza Blanca.

Mile 0.4 The bridge crossing the Rio Chama offers a good view of the river's broad, rocky floodplain. Heavy spring snowmelts have often caused the river to shift its course, which in the past, forced farmers to repair the headgates of their ditches. Although most of the headgates are now concrete, the Plaza Blanca Community Ditch headgate, located a mile south of the bridge, is still made of rocks and boughs, and often requires repair after high waters.

Mile 1.2 The view left offers an opportunity to survey the topography of the Chama Valley. In the foreground are irrigated fields and the cottonwood *bosque*. Beyond lies the middle irrigated plateau of the Los Ojos and La Puente fields. The Parkview State Fish Hatchery is visible between the villages at the foot of the sixty foot cliffs that rise up to the upper plateau on which Ensenada and Tierra Amarilla are located. Beyond, the rugged Brazos Peaks rise to an elevation of 10,000 ft.

Mile 3.8 Turn left on New Mexico 572.

Mile 4.2 Enter the Plaza Blanca Historic District. On the right is the old school, now converted into a chapel. Across the Chama Valley to the east lies the village of La Puente, with its distinctive linear settlement pattern and irrigated fields on either side of the village. Above La Puente is the plateau on which the village of Tierra Amarilla is located.

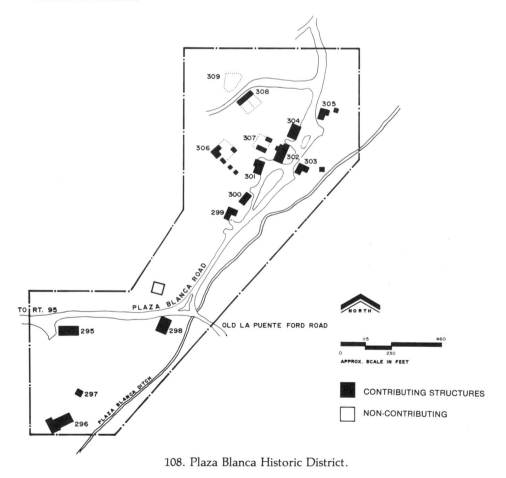

108. Plaza Blanca Historic District.

109. Ulibarri-Mercure House, built about 1885.

Mile 4.3 To the right is the ford road. Prior to the ford being washed out in a flood several years ago, residents of two villages used it to reach fields they worked on the opposite bank. Because of the family ties between the two villages, descendants often inherit farm plots in a field system other than that of their village. The contrast between the arid hillside above Plaza Blanca and the lush vegetation of the irrigated fields below indicates the important role of water in shaping the valley landscape. The *acequia* lies to the right just below the road with clumps of red willows marking its course. High grass in the middle of a field often indicates a lateral ditch, or *contra acequia*, which a farmer uses to distribute water over his entire field.

Mile 4.4 Building # 300 to the left is a good example of a single file *jacal* construction. To the right, the *acequia* rounds a cottonwood. Slightly ahead of the *acequia's* turn, a narrow field suggests how fields have been subdivided through inheritances to the point that they cannot be worked with modern, large scale farm machinery.

Mile 4.5 Take the left fork in the road.

Mile 4.6 To the left is a double post and rail corral and an unplastered *jacal* shed. To the right are several pieces of old farm equipment, including mowers, discs, and rakes, which serve as reminders of an earlier period of agricultural diversity.

Mile 4.8 Leaving the Plaza Blanca Historic District; return to Road 95.

295 La Cofradia de San Antonio de Padua de la Placita Blanca, N.M. Vernacular, about 1920, contributing. Built as school building, converted into a church about 1960.

296 Pedro Ulibarri Jr. House, N.M. Vernacular, about 1880-1910, contributing.

297 Shed, about 1910, contributing.

298 Ortega-Samora House, N.M. Vernacular, about 1900, contributing.

299 Adolfo Ulibarri House, N.M Vernacular, about 1880-1910, contributing.

300 Pedro Ulibarri-Oniel Mercure House, illustration 109, N.M. Vernacular, about 1885, contributing.

301 Frank Ulibarri Jr. House, illustration 110, N.M. Vernacular, about 1880-1910, contributing.

302 Frank Ulibarri Sr.-Johnny Valdez House, N.M. Vernacular, about 1880-1910, contributing.

303 Juan Lopez House, N.M. Vernacular, about 1880-1910, contributing.

304 Juan Ulibarri-Nicholas Lopez House, N.M. Vernacular, about 1880-1910, contributing.

305 Miguel Ulibarri House, N.M. Vernacular, about 1900-1910, contributing.

306 Frank Ulibarri Jr. Corral Complex, about 1910, contributing.

307 Frank Ulibarri Sr. Barns and Corral, N.M. Vernacular, about 1880, contributing.

308 Ulibarri-Lopez Sheds and Corral, N.M. Vernacular, about 1910, contributing.

309 Farm Equipment Graveyard, illustration 64, early twentieth-century horse drawn farm equipment: 1 thrasher, 3 reapers, 2 seed spreaders, rake, disc, 1 truck body, 1 car body, and miscellaneous wagon and implement parts, contributing.

110. Frank Ulibarri Jr. House, built about 1900.

10 — Individual Buildings and Irrigation Systems

escribed below are buildings and irrigation systems placed on the State Register of Cultural Properties and the National Register of Historic Places in 1985-87 as part of the Historic Resources of La Tierra Amarilla Parts I and II.

1   Our Lady of Lourdes Grotto, illustration 111, 20 feet east of Old Highway and 50 yards south of highway's turn into the village of Los Ojos. (See also Tour C.)

In Hispanic communities throughout northern New Mexico, religious belief historically was projected from churches into the entire environment and was given a tangible form as private chapels, shrines, temporary altars, and, in houses, as family altars and wall niches for statuary. Religious processions, most importantly Corpus Christi, annually visited these secondary sites. Chapels, shrines and temporary altars were usually sponsored by *ricos,* wealthy merchant, land and sheep-owning families.

Historically, temporary altars were erected in this area, although today none are. The Our Lady of Lourdes Grotto is the only remaining historic religious site in the area other than the churches. It commemorates Josepha Burns' escape from mishap when she lost control of her buggy and her horse raced down the steep road to Los Ojos. She attributed her survival to divine intervention. The shrine was her idea, although her children saw it to completion in 1919.

50   Casados House, illustration 112, 100 yards northwest of junction of U.S. 84 and State Rd. 95. (See also Tour C.)

This is one of the best preserved of the two-story mansions remaining in the area. This house, like the others, has an overriding symmetry of massing, full front porch, centered entrance and center hall plan with four matching square rooms on each floor. The doors, windows and balustrades are stock elements shipped in over the railroad. The segmental molding window pediments, the stick and cut-out freezes, the boxed chamfered posts and the concentration of those posts to mark the centered entrance show the hand of a local builder.

52   Sanchez-March House, illustrations 26, 27, 50 feet west of U.S. 84 and 200 yards north of State Rd. 95. (See also Tour C.)

Built about 1880, this is the best preserved of the officer's house plan houses. The type, reputed in oral tradition to have been based on an officer's house type used at Fort Lowell, introduced Anglo-American elements into the local folk tradition: symmetrical facades, centered single entrance, and the organization of the interiors for the separation of public and private space. The stock Queen Anne style elements and the wrap-around porch are features which arrived with the railroad. The barns are well-preserved examples of the two prevailing forms of log construction — hewn logs with double box notch and unhewn logs with double saddle notch.

55   Fernando Trujillo Sr. House, 50 yards west of U.S. Highway 84 and 285 yards north of State Rd. 95.

This deteriorating but largely unmodified house is an excellent example of the local hybrid folk architecture. Built about 1880, the *jacal* construction is Hispanic; the facade symmetry and chamfered porch posts Anglo-American Territorial style; and the cut-out porch brackets, folk invention.

111. Corpus Christi Celebration at the Shrine of Our Lady of Lourdes, about 1923. Photo courtesy of Aurelia Rivera.

#60 Manuelita Trujillo House, 60 feet west of U.S. Highway 84 and 200 yards south of Los Brazos River.

This is a little-modified example of the local folk building tradition at the turn of the century. The L-shaped composition of rooms as discrete units, each with its own door (and probably built in phases) and the use of adobe come from the Hispanic roots of the tradition. The orientation towards the street, gabled roof and chamfered porch post are Anglo-American introductions. The wrap-around front porch, too, is an Anglo introduction, but used in Hispanic fashion for exterior circulation.

#70 Teodoro Martinez House, 50 feet east of Hatchery Road and 150 yards north of turn off to the Hatchery. (See also Tour C, Hatchery Road Spur.)

This excellent, well-preserved example of local folk architecture was built about 1900. The single file of discrete rooms, each with its own door, is capped by a gabled roof elevated about a foot by the local use of a half-story wall.

#71 Parkview Fish Hatchery, illustration 96. (See also Tour C, Hatchery Road Spur.)

The Los Ojos Hatchery complex is the most prominent reminder of state and federal activity in the area during the 1930s. Although state and federal spending for projects like the hatchery provided local employment, the hatchery also reflected the government's development of the (once communal) surrounding mountains for recreation. So the hatchery was viewed with ambivalence locally, seen as the source of new jobs and as a symbol of the role of outside government in the loss of common lands. In the days preceding the 1967 Reies Tijerina-led raid on the County Courthouse, which brought the movement to regain control of the land grant to a head, local rumors spoke of plans to dynamite the hatchery.

—

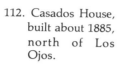

112. Casados House, built about 1885, north of Los Ojos.

The most notable aspect of the complex's design is its Beaux Arts plan. The arrangement of the buildings, their massing and fenestration is rigidly symmetrical. Ramps curve up to the main building's entrance. The eye is led from the auxiliary buildings to the higher roof of the main building, on to the monitor roof and, finally, to the 120-foot-high cliffs behind. This use of order and procession was common in government projects between the World Wars, even in one as modest and remotely located as a fish hatchery. The general plan was apparently used elsewhere in the Rockies and upstate New York. The length of the main hatchery building was varied from project to project, depending on the available water flow and local need for recreational fish.

#72 Transito Martinez Barn, 50 feet off road between Los Ojos and La Puente and 80 yards south of Hatchery turn off. (See also Tour C, Hatchery Road Spur.)

This little-modified, traditional Hispanic barn has been tree ring dated to 1912. The barn has hewn horizontal logs with double box notching and a corrugated metal gable roof with vertical planks in the gable ends. The ends of transverse interior hewn log wall are visible at the mid-point of the long side, while exposed beam ends mark loft floor.

#73, #74, #131 George Becker House, Bunk House and Barn, about 40 feet east of road between Los Ojos and La Puente and 100 yards south of Hatchery turn off.

Built in 1918 and 1919, the Becker House is among the most elaborate Bungalows built in New Mexico. Denver businessman George Becker and his wife Emma Burns Becker split their time between Denver and this house, which was built on Burns family land. The wood frame construction and self-conscious styling were as different from local adobe folk houses as their lives were from those of the nearby subsistence farmer/ranchers. The barn is the largest in the area and the only one with a gambrel roof. Its compartmentalized, horizontal log first floor and attic wall are similar to other local barns. Its extensive use of logs and nearness to the site of Fort Lowell suggest the possibility that it reuses logs from the fort. The Becker complex is completed by the Southwest Vernacular bunk house built in 1938.

#75 Officer's House, illustration 97, 175 feet east of road between Los Ojos and La Puente and 300 yards south of Hatchery turn off. (See also Tour C, Hatchery Road Spur.) Determined eligible for National Register, but not registered.

This is referred to locally as the Officer's House. It is in the general area of Fort Lowell. It was modeled on house plans used at the fort and possibly built by George Lemon, a soldier who stayed in the area after the fort was abandoned in 1869. It introduced such new elements into the local building tradition as symmetrical facades facing the street and the separation of public and private space.

76 Tony Manzanares House, 0.3 miles north of La Puente Church.

Built in the 1930s, this house indicates the continuing vitality of log construction and the local housing tradition. Tree ring samples could determine if the hewn logs were reused from an earlier building, as often happened, or cut fresh for this house, which seems unlikely at this late date. Numerous other examples of *jacal* remain from this decade. It may have begun as a one-room "honeymoon cottage."

108 Burns Lake Bungalow of the Parkview Hatchery, one-half mile south of the Hatchery.

The Burns Lake House was built as part of the 1932-34 Hatchery project, using the same materials.

109 Log House, 50 feet east of road between Los Ojos and La Puente and 230 yards south of Hatchery turn off.

This is a well-preserved, slightly-modified example of Hispanic log housing. The dovetail notching, half dovetail joints and steep roof are somewhat unusual.

134 Samuel Sanchez Barns, 80 yards southwest of the Sanchez house along private farm roadway, north of Los Brazos.

Tree ring dated after 1887, probably built by 1895, these barns with their dovetail notches are exellent examples of local builders incorporating new building techniques into traditional building styles. The proximity of these barns to the site of the original speculative town of Park View probably accounts for their use of dovetail notching. The Swedish immigrant residents of Park View introduced this notching style to the area. These barns likely reuse logs from that settlement which was abandoned shortly after 1880.

135 Samuel Sanchez House, illustration 115, 100 yards west of Highway 84 and 0.4 miles north of US 84 junction with NM 162, north of Los Brazos.

Built in the 1880's, the house employs a slightly modified officer's house plan; its many milled ornaments make it a fine local example of the Folk Territorial Style. These ornaments include molding cornices, tongue-and-groove siding on dormers, frieze boards, lathed porch posts and engaged columns with brackets.

249 Miguel Valdez Barn, illustration 42, 50 yards east of San Joaquin Church Loop Road (east) and 140 yards south of Ensenada Headgate Road, in Ensenada.

Perhaps built in the 1920's, this barn is one of the best local examples of Hispanic modular barn construction. It is one of the few shed-roofed barns in the area; most have received gabled metal roofs against the heavy winter snows. The barn consists of three rectangular modules of horizontal logs with double saddle notches.

251 San Joaquin Church, illustration 50, 100 yards east of Ensenada Road and 50 yards south of Headgate Road, in Ensenada.

Built in 1915, this New Mexico Vernacular/Gothic Revival Style church reflects the population spurt in the area prior to World War I. Several villages constructed small churches during this period. This is the only church with a detached belfry known to the authors. Only slightly larger than local houses and built with the same materials, the nave is twenty-eight feet wide, the transepts nine feet wide.

266, # 267 Ramon Jaramillo House and Barn, illustration 35, 100 feet west of Ensenada Road and 50 yards south of end of pavement.

Built in 1887, this little-modified structure with its half-story wall construction, gable balcony and milled ornaments is a premier example of the local folk building tradition. With its high ground location just above the Brazos River floodplain, the house was a landmark for designating the major turn in the Parkview Ditch as well the old ford crossing from Ensenada to Brazos.

―

113

The Community Ditches of La Tierra Amarilla

The community ditches of La Tierra Amarilla played a primary role in shaping the cultural landscape. They mark the boundary between the agricultural lands below, and the arid sagebrush and juniper-covered sandhills above, and serve as a field and property boundary which predates all fences and most roads. Through the various ditch associations, the ditches also provided village residents with their most important focus for communal obligation, organization and decision-making. Along with the church, the community ditches were the central institution of the agrarian Hispanic villages of northern New Mexico. Since the villages in La Tierra Amarilla are not incorporated, the community ditches continue to play an important role in instilling a sense of community as well as providing a vital link with the historic cultural roots of the area.

311 Tierra Amarilla Community Ditch, illustrations 59, 60. Dug in 1862 and registered in the State Engineer's Office in file # 0430, the ditch serves 75 field plots and bisects Tierra Amarilla, irrigating residential garden plots. It diverts from Rito de Tierra Amarilla 2 miles east-southeast of Tierra Amarilla, the *desagüe* (or discharge point) is 0.2 miles north of La Corridera Road, 1.7 miles west of Tierra Amarilla Courthouse. One major *contra acequia:* High Line Lateral; Total length: 4.4 miles; irrigates: 710 acres; midway dimensions: bottom width 6 feet, top width 9 feet, depth 1.5 feet.

312 Parkview Community Ditch, illustrations 54. Dug in 1862 and registered in the State Engineer's Office in file # 0477, the ditch is the longest in the area, dropping over 100 feet as it falls from the Ensenada plateau to Parkview. Oral tradition recalls a flour mill or *molina* at the ditch's steepest fall. It diverts from Brazos River in a single ditch also serving Ensenada and El Porvenir Ditches 4.5 miles east of Ensenada, the *desagüe* is 1 mile southwest of State Fish Hatchery into La Puente Community Ditch. Total length: 8.1 miles; irrigates: about 1,125 acres; midway dimensions: bottom width 6 feet, top width 8 feet, depth 1.5 feet.

313 Ensenada Community Ditch, illustrations 55, 65. Built in 1862 with additions in 1890 and 1917 and registered in the State Engineer's Office in file # 0436, the ditch is the oldest active community ditch in the area. It diverts from Brazos River in a single ditch also serving El Porvenir and Parkview Ditches 4.5 miles east of Ensenada; the *desagüe* is 0.3 miles west of US 84, 0.5 miles northeast of State Fish Hatchery. *Contra acequias:* the Cruz and Ulibarri Laterials; total length: 7.2 miles; irrigates: 982 acres; midway dimensions: bottom width 6 feet, top width 9 feet, depth 1.5 feet.

314 El Porvenir Community Ditch, illustration 67. Dug as an addition to the Ensenada Ditch about 1894 and registered in the State Engineer's Office in file # 0660, the ditch added irrigated acreage to the north side of Ensenada. It diverts from Brazos River in a single ditch also serving Ensenada and Parkview Ditches 4.5 miles east of Ensenada; the *desagüe* is 0.5 miles north of Ensenada where ditch drains back to Brazos River. Total length: 3.7 miles; irrigates: 580 acres; midway dimensions: bottom width 4 feet, top width 7 feet, depth 2 feet.

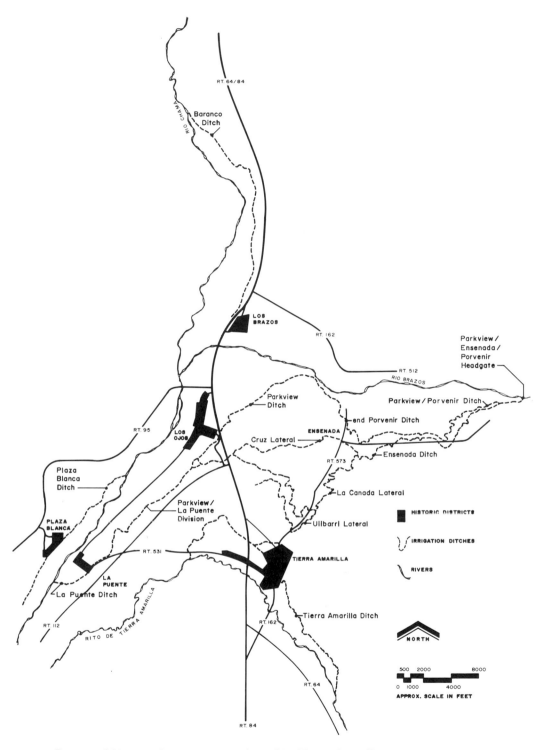

RT. 64/84

RIO CHAMA

Baranco
Ditch

LOS
BRAZOS

RT. 162

Parkview/
Ensenada/
Porvenir
Headgate

RT. 512

RIO BRAZOS

Parkview
Ditch

Parkview/Porvenir Ditch

end Porvenir Ditch

RT. 95

LOS
OJOS

ENSENADA

Cruz Lateral

Ensenada Ditch

RT. 573

Plaza
Blanca
Ditch

La Canada Lateral

Parkview/
La Puente
Division

Ullbarrl Lateral

HISTORIC DISTRICTS

PLAZA
BLANCA

IRRIGATION DITCHES

RT. 531

TIERRA AMARILLA

RIVERS

LA
PUENTE

La Puente Ditch

RITO DE TIERRA AMARILLA

RT. 112

RT. 162

Tierra Amarilla Ditch

NORTH

RT. 64

500   2000   8000

0   1000   4000

APPROX. SCALE IN FEET

RT. 84

113. Registered Historic Community Ditches of La Tierra Amarilla.

#315 Plaza Blanca Community Ditch, illustration 56. Dug prior to 1900, the ditch serves 19 plots. Efforts are being made to register the ditch with the State Engineer in order to obtain funding for a concrete headgate to stabilize the diversion. Presently the ditch employs a wooden headgate, but as the Chama River shifts its course, its more fragile headgate remains vulnerable to rock, gravel and debris buildups. It diverts from Chama River 2 miles west-southwest of State Fish Hatchery; the *desagüe* is 1 mile south-southwest of Plaza Blanca. Total length: 2.5 miles; irrigates: about 250 acres; midway dimensions: bottom width 3 feet, top width 6 feet, depth 1.5 feet.

#316 El Barranco Ditch, illustration 66. Dug prior to 1907 and registered in the State Engineer's Office in file #02566, the ditch irrigates the Chama River floodplain above Los Brazos, serving sixteen plots. It diverts from Chama River; the *desague* is at Upper Brazos Ditch. Total length: 3.8 miles; irrigates: 340 acres.

#318 La Puente Community Ditch, illustration 63. Dug as a part of the Parkview Ditch in 1862, the ditch bisects La Puente serving garden plots as well as sixteen field plots. It diverts from Parkview *desague* 100 yards southwest of State Fish Hatchery lake; the *desagüe* is 0.7 miles southwest of La Puente at the Chama River. Total length: 2 miles; irrigates: about 307 acres; midway dimensions: bottom width 4 feet, top width 6 feet, depth 1.5 feet.

114. Ditch and lateral, east of Los Brazos.

Notes

Mucho Más Antes

1. Greenlee, Robert. "Archeological Sites in the Chama Valley. "In *Report on Excavation at Tsama, 1929-1933.* Manuscript, Laboratory of Anthropology, Santa Fe. Laboratory Library separate # 651.
2. Mera, H.P. "Survey of Biscuit Ware Area in Northern New Mexico." *Laboratory of Anthropology Technical Series, Bulletin # 6.* May 15, 1931.

1 — History and Settlement Patterns

1. Warner, Ted ed. *The Dominguez-Escalente Journal.* (Provo, Utah: BYU Press, 1976), 7.
2. Richard Nostrand, "The Century of Hispano Expansion," *New Mexico Historical Review,* 62, No. 4 (October 1987), 361-67. The existence of a secondary Spanish cultural hearth in north central New Mexico has been the subject of recent, heated debate. The controversy was initiated by Richard Nostrand, "The Hispano Homeland in 1900," *Annals of the Association of American Geographers (AAAG),* 70, no. 3 (September 1980), 382-96. It attracted an extended rebuttal: J.M. Blaut and Antonio Rios-Bustamante, "Commentary on Nostrand's 'Hispanos' and their 'Homeland,' " *AAAG,* 74, no. 1 (1984), 157-164, and many other commentaries, in *AAAG,* 71, no.2 (June 1981), 280-283; 74, no. 1(1984), 164-169, 74, no. 1 (1984), 164-169, 74, no. 1 (1984), 169-171.
3. Paul Kutsche, John R. VanNess and Andrew T. Smith, "A Unified Approach to the Anthropology of Hispanic Northern New Mexico," *Historical Archaeology* 10, no. 1 (1976), 6.
4. Frances Leon Swadish, *Los Primeros Pobladores* (South Bend: University of Notre Dame Press, 1974), 39, 47, 60-61.
5. Swadish, 61-63; Victor Westphall, *Mercedes Reales* (Albuquerque: UNM Press, 1983), 127.
6. Kutsche and VanNess, 19. See also Peter Van Dresser, *Development on a Human Scale,* (New York: Praeger, 1973), 90-105; John Stilgoe, *The Common Landscape of America,* (New Haven: Yale University Press, 1982), 34-43; Alvan Carlson, "Rural Settlement Patterns in the San Luis Valley," *Colorado Magazine,* 44, no. 2 (Spring 1967), 114-119.
7. Marc Simmons, "Settlement Patterns and Village Plans in Colonial New Mexico," in David Weber, ed., *New Spain's Far Northern Frontier,* (Albuquerque: UNM Press, 1979), 103-106; Stephan de Borhegyi, "The Evolution of a Landscape," *Landscape,* 4, no. 1 (Summer 1954), 24-30.
8. Swadish, 133-138; Kutsche, VanNess and Smith, 5-7.
9. Malcolm Ebright, *The Tierra Amarilla Land Grant,* (Santa Fe: Center for Land Grant Studies, 1980).
10. Robert Torrez has uncovered oral tradition and information in land title abstracts supporting the 1860-1861 settlement dates, which will appear in his forthcoming University of New Mexico doctoral dissertation. He points to additional support for these dates, including: "Tierra Amarilla Looks Prosperous," *Santa Fe New Mexican* (December 4, 1914); Obituary, *El Nuevo Estado* (February 15, 1911). For previous discussions of the settlement date of the Tierra Amarilla grant see Swadish, 81; Westphall, 127.

—

11. Ebright, 45-49.

12. Robert Torrez, "The San Juan Gold Rush of 1860 and its Effects on the Development of Northern New Mexico," *New Mexico Historical Review*, 63, no. 3 (July 1988), 257-272.

13. Robert Torrez, " 'El Bornes': La Tierra Amarilla and T.D. Burns," *New Mexico Historical Review*, 56, no. 2, (April 1981), 161-177; Robert Torrez, "The Tierra Amarilla," 10-12, in Anselmo F. Arellano, ed., *La Tierra Amarilla: The People of the Chama Valley* (n.p.: Chama Valley Schools, 1978); Swadish, 82-83.

14. McCauley, C.A.H., *Report of the San Juan Reconnaissance of 1877*, House of Rep., 45th Cong., 3rd Session, Report of Chief of Engineers, Vol. V, Pt. III, 1767.

15. U.S. Census, *Statistics of Population*, "Counties," "Population of Civil Divisions Less Than Counties," "Minor Civil Divisions," etc, 1870-1980; U.S. Census, "Enumerator Sheets, Rio Arriba County," 1870, 1880, 1900 (microfilm, University of New Mexico Special Collections); Ebright, 45-48.

16. Ebright, 8; Westphall 127-131.

17. Ebright, 27.

18. Westphall, 127-131, 224-233; Ebright, ix-xii, 1-29; Swadish, 84-88; Robert Torrez, "La Merced de Tierra Amarilla," 32-36, in Arellano; Richard Gardner, *Grito! Reies Tijerina and the New Mexico Land Grant War of 1967*, (Indianapolis: Bobbs—Merrill, 1970), 48-65.

19. David Myrick, *New Mexico's Railroads*, (Golden, Colorado: Colorado Railroad Museum, 1970), 160-161.

20. Swadish, 103-127; Torrez, "The Tierra Amarilla," 15-16; Gardner, 68-70; Paul Kutsche and John R. VanNess *Cañones: Values, Crisis and Survival in a Northern New Mexico Village*, (Albuquerque: UNM Press, 1981), 24.

21. See Gardner for an introduction to the land grant movement, and note 18 above for the scholarly examination of the history of the grant.

22. Swadish, 127-132; Torrez, "The Tierra Amarilla," 16; Gardner; Kutsche and VanNess, 223-231.

115. Samuel Sanchez House, north of Los Brazos, built about 1885.

1. Charles Gritzner, "Log Houses in New Mexico," *Pioneer America*, 3, no. 3 (July 1971), 54-62; Charles Gritzner, "Construction Materials in a Folk Housing Tradition," *Pioneer America*, 6, no. 1 (January 1974), 25-39; "A Catalog of New Mexico Farm Building Terms," *Landscape*, 1, no. 3 (Winter 1952), 31-32; John J. Winberry, "The Log House in Mexico: Distribution, Origin and Diffusion," unpublished dissertation, Baton Rouge, LSU, 1971.

2. Bainbridge Bunting, *Early Architecture in New Mexico*, (Albuquerque: University of New Mexico Press, 1976), 10-12; Boyd Pratt, *The North Central Regional Overview*, Volume 1, (Santa Fe: Historic Preservation Division, 1988), 260-261.

3. J.B. Jackson, "First Comes the House," *Landscape*, 9, no. 2 (Winter 1959-60), 26-32; Chris Wilson, "When a Room is the Hall," *Mass* (Journal of the School of Architecture, UNM), 2 (Summer 1984), 17-23.

4. Jackson, "First Comes the House," 28-29; Wilson, "When A Room," 19-20.

5. Jackson, "First Comes the House"; Wilson, "When a Room"; Bainbridge Bunting, *Early Architecture*; A.W. Conway, "A Northern New Mexico House-Type," *Landscape*, 1, no. 2 (1951), 20-21; Bainbridge Bunting, *Taos Adobes*, (Santa Fe: Museum of New Mexico Press, 1964); Beverly Spears, *American Adobes: Rural Houses of Northern New Mexico*, (Albuquerque: University of New Mexico Press, 1986).

6. The installation was known as Camp Plummer about 1866-68 and Fort Lowell about 1868-69. Torrez, "The Tierra Amarilla," 9-10, in Anselmo Arellano ed., *La Tierra Amarilla: The People of the Chama Valley*, (Tierra Amarilla, New Mexico: Chama Valley Schools, 1978); Jerry Williams, *New Mexico in Maps*, (Albuquerque: UNM Press, 1986), 11-13; D. Mortimer Lee, "Camp Plummer, New Mexico, December 31st, 1867," plan, Records of the Office of Quartermaster General, Consolidated Correspondence File, Camp Plummer, N.M., Record Group no. 92, The National Archives, Washington, D.C.; D. Mortimer Lee, "Camp Plummer, New Mexico, July 1st, 1868," aerial view, General File, The National Archives, Washington, D.C.

7. Virginia McCallister and Lee McCallister, *A Field Guilde to American Houses*, (New York: Alfred A. Knopf, 1984), 198-203; Vincent Scully, *The Shingle Style and the Stick Style*, (New Haven: Yale University Press, 1955, revised edition 1971), figure 16, pp. xxiii-lix.

8. At first, Tierra Amarilla's most important connection with the outside world was the Old Spanish Trail, down the Chama River to Abiquiu. But from the time of the first settlements, trails out of Tierra Amarilla through the San Luis Valley were used by parties of buffalo hunters from Tierra Amarilla on their way to the plains. When the railroad reached Trinidad and Pueblo, Colorado in the early 1870s, the freight roads that developed over these early trails became the most direct connection to outside products. When the Denver, Rio Grande and Western Railroad passed through the San Luis Valley to reach Chama in 1880, the reorientation of Tierra Amarilla toward Colorado was strengthened. Only with the construction of state highways during the 1930s from Abiquiu to Tierra Amarilla, did the focus shift back toward other New Mexico communities.

9. Nicholas G. Morgan, "Mormon Colonization in the San Luis Valley," *Colorado Magazine*, 27, no. 4 (October 1950), 269-293; Richard Sherlock, "Mormon Migration and Settlement after 1875," *Journal of Mormon History*, 2 (1975), 53-68; Carleton Q. Anderson et al. eds, *The Mormons: 100 Years in the San Luis Valley of Colorado*, (n.p.: La Jara Stake, LDS, 1983).

—

10. Richard Francaviglia, *The Mormon Landscape*, (New York: AMS Press, 1978), 16-20; Richard Francaviglia, "Mormon Center-Hall Houses in the American West," *AAAG*, 61, no. 1 (1971), 65-71; Richard C. Poulsen, "Stone Buildings of Beaver City," *Utah Historical Quarterly (UHQ)*, 43, no. 3, 278-284; Teddy Griffith, "A Heritage of Stone in Willard," *UHQ*, 43, no. 2 (Summer 1975), 286-300; Thomas Carter, " 'The Best of its Kind and Grade': Rebuilding the Sanpete Valley, 1890-1910," *UHQ*, 54, no. 1 (Winter 1986), 88-112; McCallister and McCallister, *Field Guide*, 202-203; Allen Noble, *Wood, Brick, and Stone: The North American Settlement Landscape*, (Amherst: University of Massachusetts Press, 1984), vol. 1, 50-55, vol. 2, 160-162; Thomas Carter and Peter Goss, *Utah's Historic Architecture, 1847-1940*, (Salt Lake City: University of Utah Press, 1988), 16, 21-23.

11. The presence of Juan and Maria Luz Trujillo, Mormon converts, apparently from Tierra Amarilla, among the first group of settlers at Manasa suggest direct contact. See Morgan, "Mormon Colonization," 286; United States Census, "Census Enumerator Sheets for Rio Arriba County, New Mexico, 1870" microfilm, Special Collections, University of New Mexico Library, Tierra Amarilla, precinct no. 16, sheets 6-7.

12. Noble, *Wood, Brick and Stone*, vol. 2, 110-112; Francaviglia, *Mormon Landscape*, 6-7, 57; Arellano, *La Tierra Amarilla*, 95.

13. Carleton, 82-85; Morgan, 280, 283-284; Richard H. Jackson, "The Use of Adobe in the Mormon Cultural Region," *Journal of Cultural Geography* 1, no. 2 (1980), 82-95.

14. Bathrooms and kitchens containing modern utilities, which have been added since about 1925, are generally shed roofed and about evenly divided between those added on axis with the other rooms, in the traditional linear fashion, and those added to the rear of the building. The most significant factors in determining where these additions were positioned appears to have been the relationship of the building to the property line and the gradual acceptance of two-room-deep floor plans, those plans introduced through the one- and two-story four square houses.

15. Bunting, *Early Architecture*, 60-63; Bunting, *Taos Adobes*; A.W. Conway, "Southwest Colonial Farms," *Landscape*, 1, no.1 (1951), 6-9.

3 — *Land and Water Use*

1. Wells A. Hutchins, "The Community Acequia: Its Origin and Development," *Southwest History Quarterly*, 31, (January, 1928), 266.

2. Hutchins, 268.

3. Ralph Emerson Twitchell, *The Leading Facts of New Mexico History*, (Cedar Rapids, Iowa: The Torch Press, 1912), II, 176.

4. Paul Kutsche, John R. VanNess and Andrew T. Smith, "A Unified Approach to the Anthropology of Hispanic Northern New Mexico," *Historical Archeology*, 10, No. 1 (1976), 1, 6.

5. This summary of the seasonal cycle of the *acequia* is based upon several interviews with members of various community ditches in La Tierra Amarilla. For an excellent detailing of a year spent working a ditch, see Stanley Crawford, *Mayordomo*, (Albuquerque: University of New Mexico Press, 1988).

6. *Census of the United States: Agriculture, Vol. VII, 1909 & 1910*, (Washington: Government Printing Office, 1913), 146-181.

7. Malcolm Ebright, "New Mexican Land Grants: The Legal Background," and John R. Van-Ness, "Hispanic Land Grants: Ecology and Subsistence," in Charles L. Briggs and John R. VanNess, eds., *Land, Water, and Culture: New Perspectives on Hispanic Land Grants,* (Albuquerque: University of New Mexico Press, 1987), 20, 25, 190; and William deBuys, *Enchantment and Exploitation,* (Albuquerque: University of New Mexico Press, 1985), 194. Interviews with older sheepmen confirm that opening individual fields to create a communal pasture was a common practice each year in the fall.
8. Michael C. Meyer, *Water in the Hispanic Southwest: A Social and Legal History,* (Tucson: University of Arizona Press, 1984), 4.
9. Phil Lovato, *Las Acequias Del Norte,* (Taos, New Mexico: Four Corners Regional Commission, New Mexico State Planning Office, Kit Carson Memorial Foundation, Inc., 1974), 2.

4 – Learning from the Past

1. William deBuys, *Enchantment and Exploitation,* (Albuquerque: University of New Mexico Press, 1985), 195.
2. Peter vanDresser, *Development on a Human Scale: Potentials for Ecologically Guided Growth in Northern New Mexico,* (New York: Praeger Publishers, 1973), 80.
3. Hazel Henderson, *Creating Alternative Futures: The End of Economics,* (New York: Berkley Publishing Corp., 1978); Ernst F. Schumacher, *Small is Beautiful: A Study of Economics As If People Mattered,* (London: Blond and Briggs, 1973). These iconoclastic looks at planning and economic policy have provided local community activists with a theoretical basis for many of the programs they have initiated.
4. deBuys, 172, 309, 311; Donald Cutter, "The Legacy of the Treaty of Guadalupe Hidalgo," *New Mexico Historical Review,* 53, no. 4 (October, 1978), 305-315.
5. Cutter, 314; Ebright, 28; Kutsche and VanNess, 19; U.S. House of Representatives, Committee on Interior and Insular Affairs, *Status of Community Land Grants in Northern New Mexico,* 100th Congress, 2nd session, Serial 100-65, 1989.
6. deBuys, 312.
7. deBuys, 312-15.

116. In the Los Ojos Historic District.